ZOMBIE THOUGHTS AND BALLET FOR ALIENS

ZOMBIE THOUGHTS AND BALLET FOR ALIENS

2 PLAYS FOR YOUNG AUDIENCES

Jennifer A. Kokai and Oliver Kokai-Means
with Gerard Hernandez

VANDERBILT UNIVERSITY PRESS
NASHVILLE, TENNESSEE

Published 2025 by Vanderbilt University Press.

LIBRARY OF CONGRESS CATALOGING-IN-PUBLICATION DATA

Names: Kokai, Jennifer A., 1979- author | Kokai-Means, Oliver. Zombie thoughts | Hernandez, Gerard (Playwright). Ballet for aliens
Title: Zombie thoughts : and Ballet for aliens : two plays for young audiences / Jennifer A. Kokai, Oliver Kokai-Means and Gerard Hernandez.
Other titles: Zombie thoughts (Compilation)
Description: Nashville : Vanderbilt University Press, 2025.
Identifiers: LCCN 2025019222 (print) | LCCN 2025019223 (ebook) | ISBN 9780826508188 paperback | ISBN 9780826508195 epub | ISBN 9780826508201 pdf
Subjects: LCSH: Anxiety disorders--Juvenile drama | Diseases--Juvenile drama | LCGFT: Drama
Classification: LCC PS3611.O53 A6 2025 (print) | LCC PS3611.O53 (ebook) | DDC 812/.6--dc23/eng/20250520
LC record available at https://lccn.loc.gov/2025019222
LC ebook record available at https://lccn.loc.gov/2025019223

To Jean-Louise England,
from Ollie and Jenny

To Michael Hernandez
and Rebecca Ory Hernandez,
from Gerard

CONTENTS

Foreword

Zombie Thoughts and Ballet for Aliens: Two Plays for Young Audiences, an anthology compiled by Jenny Kokai and containing two plays co-written with her then-nine-year-old son Oliver Kokai-Means and Gerard Hernandez, is a work that gives the reader a glimpse into the world of two individuals with two different disabilities. This anthology is close to my heart because I am also a theater artist with a disability and I have dedicated my life's work to ensuring that people with disabilities have a voice in their theater making. Kokai's contribution creates a reproducible framework that centers individuals with disabilities in the creation of a play. These sorts of frameworks are deeply needed within the world of Theater for Young Audiences (TYA) as well as in the spheres of theater education, special education, and the general educational classroom.

There is nothing comparable to witnessing the transformational power of the art form of TYA when experienced by a young person. Throughout my twenty-five-year career, I have experienced this numerous times as an actor, director, and producer. I will unpack three experiences here.

To navigate the world—and act on stage—I wear forearm crutches. I spend a great deal of time thinking, testing, and refining how the crutches can become an extension of my character. When I use the word *extension*, I am not talking about altering the dialogue or the playwright's original intention so that extra attention can be brought to the crutches. I am melding the character and crutches into one being. I cannot separate myself from my crutches and neither can the character I am portraying.

When I played Conrad (one of the two children left at home on a rainy day by their mother in Katie Mitchell's adaptation of *The Cat in the Hat*), I had to consider how my character might use the crutches since the nature of disability means that I cannot leave them off stage. In the play, the Cat makes an enormous mess simulated by giant foam balls in the children's home which must be cleaned up. When I worked in the rehearsal room collaboratively with the director and choreographer to achieve their vision, we spoke at length about this very crucial moment in the play. How will Conrad quickly clean up this mess before mom gets home and avoid getting in trouble? We worked with the sound designer to adjust the speed and tempo of the background music as I got on my knees to sweep and organize the balls into piles. When the Cat returns with her giant machine to clean the room "even FASTER," the Cat easily finishes the job.

The Cat in the Hat is not a play about a little boy on crutches cleaning a house before mom comes home. But I am an actor who uses crutches and I can't do my job without them. Throughout the run of this play, there were several occasions when kids with disabilities requested to talk to me after the show. These young people had never seen someone who looked like them on stage. They were keenly interested in knowing how I got my start in theater. After talking to me, many decided that they wanted to start taking acting classes as I had done. Their families later shared with me that this experience had inspired their children's journey into exploring theater. Representation matters. The character of the boy in *The Cat in the Hat* was not originally envisioned with crutches in the book or play, but was given a new dimension when embodied by an actor who navigates the world in a different way.

As a director, I have always been drawn to opportunities to stage immersive theatrical experiences where the audience can literally enter into the storytelling. As part of my work as artistic director at Trike Theatre in Northwest Arkansas, I staged *Birdie and the Beanstalk* by Meg Greene, a play for preschool audiences. We invited several young theatergoers on stage to use their arms to create a bridge for two characters to walk across and then to voice sound effects to simulate the sound of walking across the bridge. Later, one of the children's parents told me that their son was mostly nonverbal, but that he had made those sounds freely on stage that day. Theater has the power to be transformational for the very young.

Finally, individuals with disabilities can find their voice participating in the theatrical process. I additionally serve as executive artistic director of Circle Theatre, a forty-year-old nonprofit that provides authentic experiences for individuals of all abilities both on and off stage in Omaha, Nebraska.

Recently we staged an hour-long production of the play *Capture the Moon*, by Ernest Joselovitz and Harry Michael Bagdasian, with sixty-five actors. This folk tale tells the story of a group of Jewish villagers plagued by darkness who go on a journey to bring the moon and its light back to their home. Our cast featured actors with disabilities in lead and supporting roles, as well as players with one line and others whose roles were completely movement based. Although it is commonly accepted that the actors with the most lines carry the story, we crafted the production so that the individuals who had just one line or choreographed movement were the pivotal characters who motivated the main characters. Without their contribution, the play could not continue. Any contribution created intentionally and with full inclusion in mind by and for individuals with disabilities is meaningful.

Jenny Kokai did not set out to write a play about disabilities. She sought to create new avenues for emerging artists with disabilities to write from their own experiences. There are very few existing initiatives within the context of Theater for Young Audiences like the one that resulted from this anthology. Kokai gave Oliver and Gerard (the then-young writers) the ability to explore the subject of disabilities in a playful and imaginative way that brings the reader into their challenges.

The exciting and inclusive plays in this new anthology are brilliant and authentic contributions to the TYA canon. They provide a window into a world of disabilities that are now given its time to flourish inside the ever-expanded tent of Theater for Young Audiences.

FRAN SILLAU, MFA
Board Member for TYA/USA and the Children's Theater Foundation of America

INTRODUCTION

"Let Them Yap"

The Process and Value of Writing Professional Theater With Young Writers

Jennifer A. Kokai
and Oliver Kokai-Means

There's a story about a spider that is essential to these plays and our process but not found anywhere in them. While brainstorming for *Ballet for Aliens* with my two young colleagues Gerard and Ollie, we found ourselves lying on the living room floor staring up. We were discussing the potential for a lightsaber battle in the play when we noticed a spider descending and climbing a web from our ceiling. We pivoted to making up a character for the spider: what its name was, what its goal was sailing up and down on that strand of web, what it thought of us. We briefly considered putting it into the play in some fashion. But we didn't.

Nevertheless the spider time was not wasted—it was practice for the kind of work playwrights need to do to create interesting characters on stage: we gave it a personality, we gave it an objective, we gave it an opinion on other people on stage with it. If I had tried to do this in a formal instructional way with my teenage co-writers, I am absolutely positive they would have done so begrudgingly at best, but because we started from a creative place where we were observing the world around us while lying on the floor and we were actually "not doing work" just playing a "game," they were happy to take part. Though this wasn't some deliberate mastermind strategy on my part, all of us were honing the skills playwrights need through fun. The spider improved the "work" we did after that, until we quit so my collaborators could shoot Nerf guns at each other. In our interview with Gerard recently, when I asked what he would tell folks who wanted to write plays with young people, he said "Let them yap. Just let them yap." What I take this to mean is the importance of making time and living in the spider moments, things that seem "irrelevant" or "off topic" but that make it feel safe and valued to share creative ideas regardless of their utility.

The two plays in this volume represent collaborations between an adult playwright (me) and two child (and now late teens) playwrights, Oliver Kokai-Means and Gerard Hernandez. Oliver, who is obviously my child, and I wrote the play *Zombie Thoughts* together when he was nine, and it was produced when he was eleven. It has gone on to be produced and toured across the US by nearly a dozen groups, played a baseball stadium, and been produced by Riverside: The National Theatre of Parramatta in Sydney, Australia. It has also inspired a phone app game and been turned into an interactive video production. Because we found our collaboration so successful, when he was thirteen we asked his friend Gerard Hernandez if he wanted to collaborate with both of us on another play, which became *Ballet for Aliens* and toured to over nineteen thousand teachers and students across Utah when the kids were fifteen.

Both plays ended up being explicitly about invisible disabilities: *Zombie Thoughts* about generalized anxiety disorder, *Ballet for Aliens* about Crohn's disease, and for both plays, ultimately also implicitly the neurodiversity of the younger playwrights. This was again not some kind of intentional goal to create plays about disability. In fact, everything you will read started from a singular goal: to write a play for professional actors to tour to young audiences with some cool young people I knew.

This introduction of yapping serves to outline the process we made up to create the plays, the now slightly less young writers' reflections on what skills they learned, what value this process holds for them, and why this matters. It will include writing from Oliver and materials from interviews with Gerard Hernandez and some formative contributors to the project. It is being written into a document primarily by me, Jenny, because my younger colleagues are busy with high school homework and college applications, and though it is just daily life for them, each is navigating those things while receiving ongoing treatments for their respective chronic conditions. All of this is ultimately in service of an argument for why professional theater for young audiences should be written by young writers, or at the very least involve them meaningfully as dramaturgs. This isn't just as a moral good for the young authors, although it was good for them, but because ultimately we argue that the work that emerges is also better—perhaps not according to adult aesthetic judgments—but for the kid audiences it is intended for.[1]

The *Zombie Thoughts* and *Ballet for Aliens* Origin Stories

In 2016 Jerry Rapier, the artistic director for Salt Lake City's Plan-B Theatre, commissioned me to write a play for their Free Educational School Tour (or "FEST"). This tour crisscrosses Utah visiting Title 1 elementary schools (those being the schools with the highest percentage of students on free or reduced lunch). I was a member of the Plan-B Playwrights Lab: the theater company's mission is to produce works by Utah writers and in support of this, holds numerous labs to encourage and develop new plays. Plan-B is a unique kind of theater, not only for its commitment to prioritizing professional work from within a community rather than looking to urban coastal playwrights, but because it is run by a gay Asian American artistic director, a singular kind of company in rather homogenous Utah. Perhaps because of Jerry's marginalized identity, he and the Plan-B team, most notably managing director Cheryl Cluff, have made a point of highlighting works by those who are often not represented in American theater—the lab is composed of numerous women over forty, it runs a writing group for BIPOC artists and a writing group for senior citizens, and it shepherds many of these works from creation through production. Plan-B invests in their playwrights and their plays and usually has a two-year development period from initial reading through production, making decisions like casting well in advance.

While I have worked with kids for many years in many capacities, including teaching playwriting and devising to all ages from preschool through senior groups, I had not ever formally written a play for young audiences.[2] When I was asked to do so, it was in a moment in which American theater was doing some long-needed reflection on who should be telling what stories. And because of this I thought to myself, I could write this play, or I could ask the person in my house who is currently nine years old to help me write a play. The latter choice, while maybe initially seeming a little harder, would not be me, so much older than an elementary audience, assuming what this audience wants or needs to see. Instead, it could be a choice that decenters my adult voice in favor of an actual kid's voice speaking to other kids. I assumed that like any other culture, there were approaches to the world, turns of phrase, and character details that I, as an outsider to kid culture, wouldn't have access to (and I was right).

So I asked Ollie if he wanted to write a play with me. Neither he nor I had any idea what play we would write or how we would do this. He's grown up going to the theater and had done some professional acting, so it wasn't like we were starting from scratch, but he had not written a play before (which I think is entirely reasonable for someone who was nine). I told Jerry that I was planning on co-writing this play with Ollie. While Plan-B had never had a child playwright before, Jerry took this in relative stride, although he did allow in a news interview that he "had no idea where it would be headed."

The Process

The very first thing we had to do was figure out what our play was going to be about. I told Ollie it could be about anything he wanted. Given his interests, I thought it could be about hedgehogs, something heavily inspired by *How to Train Your Dragon*, the history of video games, or Minecraft. I would absolutely have been ok with whatever he decided upon. Ollie is what is considered "twice exceptional": after a neuropsychological test we learned he is both gifted (which is different from high achieving) and has learning disabilities and generalized anxiety disorder. At the time he was being unintentionally homeschooled as a third grade drop out. Added to immaturity, his disabilities proved an impossible barrier for local schools who lacked the resources or refused to follow individual learning plans. Perhaps because of the impact this was having on his life, he said that he wanted to write about anxiety. I asked him if he was sure, because as an adult this felt like a very personal and potentially shameful thing to disclose. I was also honestly worried about being perceived as exploiting him by making this the topic of a play. But he didn't see it that way. He was very matter of fact in assuring me it wasn't embarrassing; he felt nothing about it other than it was a part of his daily life and just a part of him. This was an important lesson to me, that shame around these issues is imparted by the grown-up world onto kids (this was something Gerard would later echo about discussing his own medical issues).

Once we had a topic, Ollie recalls the process like this:

> Creating *Zombie Thoughts* and later *Ballet for Aliens* was a surreal experience. As a nine-year-old, it wouldn't be surprising to say I had never done anything like it before, and as a result my knowledge of how to create a world was lacking. I spent many hours, days, and weeks with my mom figuring out how all of it should go. One of the things that developed first from this project was a method of working that both of us benefited from. What we settled on was a system where we would hang out, on walks with our dogs or in our living room, and I would act out what I thought things should be like while my mom took notes and wrote dialogue.
>
> While rare, there were things we both did together, and one of my most favorite would be the jokes. While my mom did make most of them, a lot of the jokes we created together and workshopped, and it was always amazing to hear people loved our jokes we created together. Creating different aspects was one thing I especially loved. The idea to create an animal "sidekick" was something we created together, and we refined it from a sheep to eventually a pig, purely because we could think of more pig-related puns. The locations they visited mostly came from me, however.
>
> An early step was a Pinterest mood board of my greatest fears (as you can guess it was just a joy to create) that we eventually assigned locations to, or just creatures. Whether it was a spooky ghost town, or a demonic dog hunting Sam and Pig in the shadows, everything they faced was a real thing I was, and for some of them still am, afraid of. One of the things that I like about it that doesn't always translate to the audience is how we upped the stakes, we simply ranked everything I was afraid of and followed it from bottom to top. This resulted in a really easy-to-follow increase in difficulty as they went—obviously a shark or vampire bats are more dangerous than an empty mountain, even if it is really tall.[3]

Ollie is right. Most of our work was done in short bursts of thirty to forty-five minutes and usually while doing something physical at the same time, like walking dogs or rolling around on the ground. I found it important not to confuse my expectations of what "focused" work looks like for an adult with what kind of work was most productive for our writing team. It was also a series of short tasks like the Pinterest board where I asked him to follow up on something he mentioned (like a list of fears) with a way to brainstorm on those fears in a short, easily achievable task.

We worked on the play around three times a week initially, in these short bursts, and the ideas we liked would carry over into the next conversation and less successful ideas would naturally be discarded. We essentially iterated on ideas slowly over time, like a snowball gaining mass as it rolled down a hill. Eventually we settled upon the video game structure (Ollie's idea), which gave us a way to shape our ideas into a play using the dramaturgy of a video game: starting with introducing and equipping the characters, playing through different levels, the "big boss," and then the conclusion. Ollie really liked the idea that this gave the audience an active way to participate in the journey of the play, as his experience as an avid young theatergoer was having a lot of questions and a lot of energy and me constantly shushing him and telling him we would discuss later.

Because Ollie did not feel beholden to notions of what good playwriting was, we made bold choices. The first thing we chose was that the two protagonists should memorize both parts so that the audience could truly choose which character each avatar would embody. He was totally fine with writing a scene that audiences might never experience. He had no qualms about being brutally honest about his fears, his personal failings, or the times he was not his best self. He was totally fine with the potential mayhem of letting audience members "kill" the characters and bring them back to life—he thought that was hilarious. As much as possible I let the spirit of anarchy reign, only occasionally mentioning we ought to write a note for the grown-ups in case they wanted to make the play fit a specific amount of time or account for other practical considerations.

Originally we had been told we could have three actors, and so we wrote the version of the play included in this volume, where the machine is a separate character and actor. That is our favorite version. The first table read with actors in the Plan-B lab was with the three performers playing Sam, Pig, and the Machine. We invited licensed clinical social worker

Gennie Tucker to that reading, which turned out to be really important. It was extremely helpful to have her support, as a recognized expert, to bolster that it was developmentally appropriate and acceptable for kids to talk about scary things, things that they were deeply afraid of, and to encounter those things in the theater. Later in this introduction, we will talk about why it is so important for kids to write plays for kids, professionally and not just in the classroom, and the paternalistic impulses of adults are a huge part of it. We were fortunate to have Tucker there to soothe adult fears and discomfort about childhood development.

That first reading was a huge success with the other writers in the lab offering positive and sincere feedback and addressing Ollie directly with that feedback and not just me. This was something that Ollie had had concerns about:

> Something I worried about a lot while I was making *Zombie Thoughts* and *Ballet for Aliens* and especially after I put them out there was that people wouldn't take me seriously. I was nervous that as a nine-year-old, directors and producers would assume my mother had done all of the work and was giving me credit because I was her child. After the release though I was happy to find that not only did people take me seriously, they gave me just as much credit as they did my mother.

Treating the young playwrights with dignity was something the Plan-B Company excelled at. As Jerry said, "We had to be open to explaining everything and assuming nothing." The first reading went so well, in fact, that I warned Ollie not to assume all first read throughs of a play would be that successful. That said, he was essentially horrified after the reading to discover that we weren't done and that we need to do revisions based upon the feedback.

One major note was that Jerry asked us to cut down to only two actors, which I admit to being completely and totally stumped by. I will never forget the feeling when, sitting in my office at work and discussing the problem, Ollie said "Oh! We'll just give them a phone with an app and they can read off the phone what the app is saying they have to do! Kids use apps all the time!" It was a brilliant suggestion and indicative of the problem solving and critical thinking we had been practicing throughout our journey.

Repeating the Process, This Time with Aliens

After the success of *Zombie Thoughts*, Ollie and I were motivated to repeat the process. As he had found the experience so empowering it occurred to us that his friend Gerard Hernandez might be equally interested in writing about his own circumstances. Gerard and Ollie had been on the same youth soccer team when they were small and then we remember Gerard disappearing. After a series of complicated medical tests involving traveling to remote hospitals, Gerard was diagnosed with Crohn's disease. We knew through his mother Rebecca's social media that he was having to undergo monthly infusions to keep the disease under control and that it was deeply impacting all aspects of his life including school and his then first love, ballet. We pitched to Jerry Rapier at Plan-B that we write a new FEST play with Gerard as a contributor, and because the previous collaboration had been a success, it wasn't a hard sell.

We kept much the same strategies for our writing process, as indicated by the spider story that begins this introduction. We would "work" in short bursts of forty-five minutes at most, talking about Gerard's experience, asking him questions, coming up with ridiculous ideas and things we wanted to see on stage. The list evolved but included ballet, comedy, fighting of some kind, true but bizarre anecdotes about Gerard's life (like the repeated house fires), the comforting items he wanted while going through an infusion, the things he wanted other people to know about living with Crohn's disease.

Gerard echoed Ollie's initial preference for generating material over the translation of that to the page. He said, "the actual writing part was not my thing at the time. But the ideas, that was fun. I loved coming up with the ideas and kind of how we formatted the whole thing." While it was also easier for Ollie to improvise dialogue and scenes and have me write them down for *Zombie Thoughts*, by the time we wrote *Ballet for Aliens* he felt comfortable taking the keyboard and writing his own dialogue and scenes. He additionally felt a sense of mentorship to Gerard who was a first time playwright. We had created a sort of apprenticeship system where a first-time playwright focused on ideas and improvisation and a more experienced young playwright crafted dialogue on the page.

Like in *Zombie Thoughts*, initial ideas led to a planned structure—in this case the experience of flipping through channels while trapped in a chair for eight hours receiving medical treatment. This gave us a constantly shifting world with different parodic styles, which mimicked the authors' attention spans and allowed for all of the disparate elements they determined they wanted to see.

Unlike Ollie, Gerard was less concerned about people not attributing his work to him, but since his background was ballet and not theater, he was less sure what to expect in a rehearsal room. He recalls: "I was a little nervous going into it at first because I had no idea what to expect. And I just met a bunch of new people and I was just a little bit scared. But after a little while, I felt good and comfortable. And everybody was really nice. So, yeah, really fun."[4]

The process of revision was the hardest struggle for both writers in both plays. The initial drafting process took a long, deliberative time, but they assumed once the draft was done they were done. This was not the case. As Ollie says,

> My least favorite part of creation is editing. I am fine putting words on a page and coming up with ideas, but editing down those words and changing what I said is the worst. One of the things I had to learn writing *Zombie Thoughts* and carrying over to *Ballet for Aliens* was that as long as the plays were popular I was never done. Directors wanted to ask if we could change certain things, I had to edit or remove parts, all of it continued well past when I had initially thought I was done. I did also learn that it was okay to say no though. Directors didn't always agree with certain parts and while sometimes their changes were valid and we made them, sometimes they were just not, so I had to stand my ground and say no.

This was by far the most valuable part of having an adult on the team. I could hold in my head the entirety of the script, understand the notes we were given and what they were asking, and remind the other playwrights of our ultimate purpose. Gerard, for example, would often lose track of the fact that the play depicted a twelve-year-old version of himself on his second ever transfusion. Gerard had grown accustomed to infusions and had more life experiences since then and started to criticize Jacob for not being a representation of Gerard of that day. I was able to remind him to put himself back in the shoes of a kid entirely new to this experience. My ultimate purpose as an author / script continuity expert / dramaturg is echoed in Jerry's note: "It's valuable to have an adult on the playwriting team with kid playwrights to keep the process focused and moving forward. But it has to be an adult whose only agenda is helping kids tell their stories." From the start, no doubt made easier because I was working with kids I was deeply invested in, I had to put my ego and my own impulses aside and let the plays be what they wanted them to be. I had to truly view us as a team, to take the notes they wrote down during readings seriously, to cut lines they decided didn't speak to them.

What We Learned from This

Often, writing or playwriting with kids is intended solely for educational settings. It is imagining kids writing and perhaps performing plays in a classroom. While there are other models where professional actors or companies undertake works by young writers, they are much more rare. There is no doubt that writing and performing plays in a classroom is educational, and this is echoed when Ollie and Gerard say that they felt like they grew as writers. Ollie said,

> One of the things I remember from the process was my own evolution when it came to writing dialogue. At the beginning I would contribute ideas and themes, but most of the dialogue came from my mom and I would say what I liked or didn't like. As time went on, I remember getting much more involved in the direct writing process—with *Zombie Thoughts* I can recall taking my mom's laptop when we had to do revisions and just writing parts of the script on my own. *Ballet for Aliens* made this especially obvious, unlike my involvement in much of *Zombie Thoughts*' creation, I had a much more direct addition to the written content of the play. That was one of the things I've taken away from writing both of the plays, I've been told often that I am pretty good at writing dialogue between two characters that feels natural, and I owe that to *Zombie Thoughts* and *Ballet for Aliens*, the two really introduced me to the thought processes required to make completely fictional characters talk about something new.

The two young writers also reflected on the value of having an extended project and what it taught them about persistence. Gerard commented, "I thought it was going to take like six months. That was my original thought. I was like, Oh, this is just, this is, I thought long-term project meant like half a year. No, I was not prepared whatsoever for how long that was going to take. Now I understand what a long-term project is." So while the extended development process was occasionally quite frustrating and mind-blowing (it essentially worked out to a third of Ollie's life at one point, and Sam and Pig have now been touring with *Zombie Thoughts* for half of his life), that time was beneficial both in allowing us the time we needed to work and in cultivating habits to undertake long term goals.

However, Ollie and Gerard also reflect back on valuable things they learned that wouldn't have come from a classroom experience but only through working with a professional theater. Ollie writes,

> In particular, talking to adults on their own level and having to come to agreements over different things was very helpful. As a kid it can very easily feel like all of the adults in your life have total power over you, and disagreeing or arguing is simply not allowed. The process of writing and editing *Zombie Thoughts* and *Ballet for Aliens* gave me a chance to speak to adults at an equal footing; I had at least partial ownership of the material being discussed and so the adult I was discussing with had no ability to just tell me no, if they wanted to make a change it had to go through me, and I think that really helped me when it came to feeling confident talking to adults and knowing what I had to say mattered too.

Gerard echoed this, saying:

> I feel like it was all really valuable. The experience mostly, not just like the play part of it, but, meeting everybody and actually learning how the process of producing a play works and how everybody works together, how everyone does their job specifically. And it was really, really cool to see all the behind the scenes and how everything worked in tandem.
>
> Another important idea I took away from this was better learning how to be professional. In day-to-day life professionalism is a really vital skill, and working on *Zombie Thoughts* and *Ballet for Aliens* meant I had to be respectful and employ professionalism when I was talking to directors, actors, and pretty much everyone involved in the process. Just because I was a kid didn't mean I could act like one, and if anything, it made being professional even more important, because if I wanted to be taken seriously I had to prove that I was just as much of a

> professional as they were. Oftentimes it was hard, long days of revision meant it was tough to continue to be courteous to other people when they were requesting more changes, but I had to work to remind myself that they were under no obligation to work with me, and if I couldn't be professional they could simply leave.

This was one of the places it was also helpful to have an adult on the playwriting team—while nobody at Plan-B ever got offended, I did occasionally have to explain the roles in a theatrical production and how, while Plan-B might be graciously consulting them on some matters, the sound design was not our responsibility and we weren't the boss of it.

What Adults Get Wrong and Why This Matters

GERARD: Like if you have a kid writing a play and you have an adult writing a play, two completely different things are going to come out of it. Even if they're on the same subject, same topic, same everything, like it's going to still be two completely different subjects or products in the end.

OLLIE: A lot of the stuff that's made for kids doesn't seem like it's made for kids. It's made to appeal to the people who want stuff made for kids. A lot of the TV shows aimed at children are actually just appeasing the fifty-year-old marketing people who want good products pushed out and they don't actually apply to children. Whereas if you get kids involved, they can actually say, no, I don't really want this.

JENNY: Yeah. Like what's something in the play that you think would not have been in there if an adult had written it by themselves?

GERARD: Definitely, definitely the syringe fight.

JENNY: Yeah, probably. That's probably right.

OLLIE: Yeah. Too intense. The lightsaber syringe fight.

GERARD: I mean, what kid doesn't want to see a syringe fight? That's my question.

JENNY: With kazoos.

GERARD: Oh yeah. With kazoos. With kazoos.

Like I said, I presumed that there would be elements of "kid culture" that were just as unknown to me as any other culture I am not indigenous to. This turned out to be really true. This was not just slang phrases that alienated or confused adult audiences, but also character details. For example, the director of the Australian production of *Zombie Thoughts* asked us if he could change the reference to *Minecraft* in the script to *Fortnite*, as it was his perception that the latter was currently more popular with kids than the former. I asked Ollie for his thoughts and he said no. Some kids play *Minecraft*, some kids play *Fortnite* (and yes, some play both), but this isn't incidental. The games are very different and appeal to different types of kids. He felt it was a character choice that would tell kids something about who Sam was. This was not something either I or the director knew.

Adults also didn't want the play to be "too scary" for kids. Thank heavens the initial table reading of the script in the Plan-B Lab had mental health expert Gennie Tucker present, who quickly put to rest these well-meaning fears, arguing that kids need to imaginatively experience or act out scary things to give them the resilience to deal with them in the "real world" and that the play was indeed developmentally appropriate. Although I will note the inherent oddness in a group of adults telling a kid that the play he wrote was too scary for other kids. This "too scary" idea would come up again and again in productions—with the notable exception of a middle school production in Honolulu. Ollie writes,

> The final boss, my fear presented as a goblin mask but really about something happening to my parents, is the most dangerous of all, and what I am most afraid of. This increase in stakes was something directors really struggled with, we had many a director claim the goblin mask or demon wolf were "too scary" for kids and we needed to tone them down, even though when given the choice the kids [in the middle school production] always made the goblin mask as scary as they possibly could and loved it every step of the way.

It *matters* that productions by adults for kids wanted to soften the scary elements and make them more palatable and that a group of middle schoolers doing the show picked the creepiest wolf and goblin masks they could find. It demonstrates the paternalism that so often unfortunately creeps into the choices adults make for theater for youth, and it denies kids developmentally appropriate opportunities to practice mental-health coping skills in what they are completely aware is make believe. While some kids might indeed be scared, I am not positive that it is an entirely bad thing to experience make-believe fear, and I'm not sure that safer choices are about protecting kids as much as they are protecting oneself from adult complaints.

Another company wanted to change the character of Sam's fear of "something happening to his parents" because not all kids have parents. This is an understandably inclusive impulse. However, their solution was to change it to "something happening to my teacher." While we generally love teachers in our house, as we discussed, school and Ollie were a bad combination for many years and many of his teachers made it plain to him that they did not like him and did not want him in their classroom. We had to tell these folks that not every child has a positive relationship with school or teachers, particularly if they are disabled, and that this was accidentally as exclusionary as using parents. We felt kids could extrapolate Sam's fear from the specificity of parents to mean "a grown-up who makes them feel safe."

While each of these requested changes came from a place of love and care, it is interesting that the adult production companies repeatedly thought they knew better what would work for a child audience than the child who wrote the play. This is the difficult set of extra burdens works for young audiences and young playwrights bear—while adults are allowed to creatively write about their lived experience and it is art, there are moralistic didactic expectations for theater for young audiences that are coupled with an implicit assumption that an adult knows more than a child in all cases. This led to requests for changes that inadvertently went beyond things like localizing (root beer floats do not exist in Australia, for example, so changing that detail makes sense) and fundamentally altered the characters themselves. This impulse to correct is even more troubling when young people are writing about lived experience with disability. In the case of wanting to change *parent* to *teacher*, research repeatedly demonstrates that students with disabilities are discriminated against by principals and teachers in the school system (this is an intersectional issue—BIPOC children with disabilities face even greater discrimination in schools, making avoiding the "teacher" as the referenced trusted loved one even more important). Asking a child with a disability who experienced this discrimination first-hand to change the loved one in the script to be a teacher was unintentionally cruel. Let them yap. Let them be the experts on their own lived experiences. Even if that scares you.

The Impact of the Plays

Ultimately, while I can stress how great and important this process was to the young writers and myself, the big takeaways also have to include the aesthetic achievements of the plays and the impact they had. It is not lost on me that both of these plays were not only from actual kids, which is not a large percentage of professional playwrights, but both were from kids dealing with disabilities, which is also a significantly underrepresented group of writers. Sharah Meservy, the educational coordinator for Plan-B, notes,

> Especially with *Zombie Thoughts* that I got to tour with it, we had a lot of both kids and educators that would come up and talk to us afterward. I remember Katie [Jones Nall, one of the original performers] saying that a little boy came up to her and said, "That was me. You were being me on stage." And so many teachers said, oh, so many people said, "So many of my students this year are struggling with anxiety. This has been huge." And then with *Ballet for Aliens*, getting comments through the teacher survey link where, like, there was one teacher who her son had Crohn's, and she was talking to him about it. And she said that he, you know, really resonated with it. And I think she even had him do, like, a Q and A with her class, talking about his experience after they'd seen the play. And, with *Ballet* for in the post show, an explanation of what an invisible illness or an invisible disability is. And we had comments from students that were like, "I have an invisible disability," or that would volunteer during the post show or put their hands up, which is just really cool, getting that personal connection and having them feel seen and represented.

I have no doubt that a big part of this came from having kid writers, because when I asked Gerard about writing about his disability and if it made living with it easier, he said "I mean, I already felt pretty good about my situation in the first place, because I've just been living with it for a long time. So it didn't really change anything, but it just felt good to help kind of express some of that stuff." For the young authors, this wasn't a play with a moral or a lesson or an inspirational purpose like it might have been in a different kind of children's play dealing with disability. It was literally just a play about their daily lives.

Plan-B collected comments at the shows as well as from teachers in feedback forms. Some of our favorite comments about *Zombie Thoughts* include:

> [One quiet boy said to Katie] I really related to this. Thank you. I needed it.
>
> That was the best play I've seen since I was two, and I'm nine now. Sam was my favorite character, and I don't know why she doubted herself. I really liked when she defeated the witch [we assume he meant The Machine] by being nice.
>
> I wasn't really prepared for how it made me feel. I remember feeling all those same anxieties when I was a kid, but my parents never talked to me about it. Now I have a fourteen-year-old daughter who's going through it. She says all those same things that Sam said—I'm stupid, everybody hates me. I wish she'd been here to see this.

And some of our favorite *Ballet for Aliens* comments were:

> That was an amazing play. I thought it was cool that the playwrite wrote about his expierences with Crohn disease and how he delt with it. I think the play was a great way to see you can't juge someone by their appearnce. [*sic*]
>
> I really enjoyed the play 'Ballet for Aliens' that you put on. It was very informational and I think it helped other people to respect each other. Also it was a very very funny topic to chose from. It also helped us learn new words that we didn't know. So you guys did excelent and I think if everyone saw it they would like it to. You guys did a good job of acting and staying in charictar. You all spoke very clearer that was easy to understand. And I also liked that you made us the laugh track it was very fun. [*sic*]

I asked Ollie and Gerard to reflect on the plays and their experiences from the now remote age of seventeen. Ollie wrote:

> *Zombie Thoughts* and *Ballet for Aliens* both meant a lot to me. Since *Zombie Thoughts* was more of a reflection of myself, I think it had a bigger impact on my own life, but *Ballet for Aliens* definitely

had an impact too. The first thing I think of when I consider what the two plays meant to me was how it felt when we got emails and letters from people who watched it. Hearing how much of an effect it had on kids and adults who watched it is something I am extremely happy about. I made *Zombie Thoughts* to help others who were struggling with anxiety, whether directly or by better teaching the adults in their lives what it was like, and hearing that it did just that for so many kids is amazing. I think *Zombie Thoughts* and *Ballet for Aliens* absolutely changed me for the better, the creation of the two was really amazing and both helped me with my own struggles. *Zombie Thoughts* taught me things about my own anxiety I hadn't considered, and often Sam was an example to me just like many other kids. *Ballet for Aliens* has helped me face my own fear of needles and I'm grateful for that. The creation process also, while unfortunately was impacted by the pandemic quite heavily, and I think working with my mom and Gerard on the play was often a distraction from the negativity that everyday life was during that period.

On a day-to-day basis though, *Zombie Thoughts* and *Ballet for Aliens* haven't had that much of an impact on my life. It sounds weird considering everything I just said, but I still go to high school, get my work done, and hope I get into a good college. I also happen to have written some successful plays. *Zombie Thoughts* in particular feels very strange, it's a little weird to go about my day knowing a nine-year-old version of me at what is often my worst is out there for kids and parents to watch while I do my own things. I don't often think about it, but when I do, I'm struck by how cool and unusual it is for [there to be] a young version of me out there perfectly preserved for the express purpose of helping others. I love it, don't get me wrong, but it also does make me feel weird sometimes to think about it.

Gerard also says,

> It feels, obviously it feels cool, but it's not good to talk about it because that's bragging. I mean, it depends. It's not that it's not cool to talk about. It's just not something that really comes up. Like bringing it up out of nowhere feels like bragging. Unless somebody asks, "Hey, what's one of the coolest accomplishments you've ever done?" Yeah. Then I'll probably say that.

Conclusion

In the process of writing this introduction about our experience, I asked everyone what they would tell a theater company that wanted to develop work with kids.

GERARD: Let the kid talk. Like, just let them yap for a little while, because that's where you're gonna learn, I feel like, the most stuff. If you go and try and prod them and try and ask questions and just start off like strong, they're gonna probably feel really uncomfortable around you. But if you just let them talk about whatever they want to at first, they're gonna feel so much, it's gonna be so much easier to have them talk to you about the stuff that they're gonna write the play about or whatever they're going through. So just let them talk about what they wanna talk about. Yeah, because we—we kind of just—we just kind of hung out.

JERRY: Don't be stupid and just do it. And don't assume you know more than they do. Because you don't.

OLLIE: No one understands kids better than kids themselves, so the best children's play you can write can only be done with the help of children.

And finally, I would say, as the playwright: it was a gift to be asked to write a play that would go out to tens of thousands of school kids. It's the largest potential audience for my ideas I have ever had in my life. But I could never have come up with *Zombie Thoughts* or *Ballet for Aliens* on my own. I could never have made the jokes that kids died laughing at that frankly I once wouldn't have understood; I wouldn't have created the nontraditional structures they instantly leapt to; I could never have experienced anything as good as seeing an audience of kids treat Ollie like a celebrity when we came to see a school performance and then seeing his response; I can't compare any feeling I've felt as a writer to the pride I experienced watching the kids talk to the media or school teachers and administration about their work and their ownership over it. Even though I had to cultivate patience and selflessness, and put aside my own ego and my own ideas, I do not regret it for a moment, and I am so grateful to have worked with a theater that was also willing to take a big leap and treat young writers with the seriousness they deserve and as the artist peers they are. If the work we wanted to put out there was truly in service of the kid audience we claimed it was for, having authentic voices speaking to their peers about real issues was the best possible thing we could do.

Notes

1. There is a vibrant and thriving community of professional artists passionately devoted to theater for young audiences, and so this document is not claiming to have wholly invented a new process nor dismissing or denigrating previous work in this area. It is offering another example and argument in a conversation that, judging from what is most often produced for young audiences, still really needs to be heard. Or if you know this part already, skip to the plays.
2. Devising is the process of generating a script or a performance with material created by the performers and director together.
3. I would like to note you can tell the maturity leap from the original writing of the play to now by the fact that he is analyzing the "stakes" and rising action of the play.
4. Quotes have been edited slightly to eliminate repetition. We'd like to thank Jerry Rapier and Sharah Meservy very much for their interviews, which helped us write this introduction.

ZOMBIE THOUGHTS

Jennifer A. Kokai and Oliver Kokai Means

ORIGINAL COMMISSIONED PRODUCTION HISTORY

Originally commissioned by Plan-B Theatre for their 2019 school tour

Originally performed by Katie Jones Nall and Alicia Washington

Designed by Arika Schockmel

Education Coordinator / Stage Manager, Sharah Meservy

Directed by Cheryl Cluff

CHARACTERS

The Machine Controls the world. Can shape shift. Plays every character besides SAM and PIG.

Sam Our hero. Gender is not important (adjust pronouns to the actor). Nine years old. Has an anxiety disorder and sometimes get depressed. Tries to be brave, but often fails. Gets upset and frustrated easily. Smart with words but not always smart with emotions.

Pig Sam's friend and sidekick. A wacky pun-telling pig.

STAGING NOTES

There is also a two-person version of this script without THE MACHINE. Additionally, groups wanting to perform it with more actors have chosen to have new actors come in as avatars for SAM and PIG in each level and when they die. Others have given THE MACHINE assistants or broken up their parts as well. The great thing about avatars is you can have as many as you want as long as the audience knows they are SAM or PIG or THE MACHINE in that moment.

SETTING

We are in a video game. It is also life. The levels get harder and harder and you don't get to quit playing.

Note: The two actors who play SAM and PIG should know both characters' dialogue. They should be able to do both parts. The audience plays a big part in selecting how things go.

THE MACHINE is the voice on stage and controls the play's actions. It is THE MACHINE's job to make sure the play runs on time. THE MACHINE has phrases to use if things get off course.

THE MACHINE can tell the players [the audience]:

- "You have temporarily been locked out and the game is on autopilot," or,
- "For temporal adjustment reasons the game is skipping to level [x]."

Note: This script has been reviewed and endorsed by a licensed clinical social worker and licensed behavioral analyst for its depiction of and treatment suggestions for generalized anxiety disorder.

TUTORIAL

[Zippy music, like the theme song to Pokémon *or* Zelda. *Something that tells us we are on an adventure. The two actors stand on stage, frozen. The voice is not "on stage" but is there, perhaps dressed in black like a bunraku puppeteer.]*

THE MACHINE

Welcome players to *Zombie Thoughts*. First you must choose your avatars. There are two avatars available. Raise your hand if you want Avatar A to be Sam. Raise your hand if you want Avatar B to be Sam. Avatar [A/B] you have been chosen to be Sam. Avatar [A/B] you will be Pig.

SAM

Yes! I'm the main character!

PIG

Wait what? I'm who?

THE MACHINE

Your name is Pig.

PIG

Like, oink, oink?

THE MACHINE

Yes.

PIG

This is very disappointing. I wanted to be Sam.

SAM

Maybe they'll choose you to be Sam next time?

PIG

Ok.

SAM

You're a very attractive Pig.

PIG

Am I?

SAM

Oh yes. Very.

PIG

Well, ok then.

THE MACHINE

Players, there are three choices for Sam's hat. Choose: baseball cap, cowboy hat, or top hat. Do you vote for baseball cap? Cowboy hat? Top hat? You have chosen [baseball/cowboy/top] hat.

SAM

Oh. I wear [baseball/cowboy/top] hats?

PIG

Seems like it!

SAM

I didn't know I was the kind of person who could pull this off.

THE MACHINE

Sam, you are a nine-year-old human. Abilities: intelligence, creativity, communication. Weaknesses: anxiety, irritability, moody. Equipment: book.

[PIG *hands* SAM *a book.*]

SAM

Um . . . I'm moody? I'm not moody. What does moody even mean?

THE MACHINE

Pig, you are the sidekick. Abilities: cheerfulness, empathy . . .

PIG

Very good looking.

THE MACHINE

Very good looking. Players do you want Pig to wear a giant flower headband, a fedora, or a great deal of blue eye shadow? You have chosen [headband / fedora / blue eye shadow].

PIG

I didn't think I could get any better looking, but I was wrong. The players are the best!

SAM

I don't know. I'm worried that this hat is not going to be very helpful. And what do you do with a book?

PIG

Oh, you worry too much.

SAM

I do? I guess I do. I'm concerned about my character traits.

THE MACHINE

Pig. Weaknesses: silliness, inability to focus, habit of telling bad puns. Equipment: a rubber chicken.

[PIG *gets a rubber chicken.*]

PIG

I can't see how any of those things could be weaknesses.

THE MACHINE

Players. Choose your first location. You can choose Mount Doom or Whisperrun Ghost Town. Raise your hand if you choose Mount Doom. Raise your hand if you choose Whisperrun Ghost Town.

[*If the audience chooses* Mount Doom, *continue with* You Have Chosen Mount Doom *(page 26) for the rest of the tutorial; if they choose* Whisperrun Ghost Town, *continue with* You Have Chosen Whisperrun Ghost Town *(page 28).*]

YOU HAVE CHOSEN MOUNT DOOM

THE MACHINE

You have chosen Mount Doom. Advance Sam and Pig to Mount Doom.

SAM

Wait. What?

PIG

You heard her, let's get going.

SAM

To Mount Doom? Um. I'm too tired today to go hiking.

PIG

I don't think we have a choice. The players pick and we have to do what they say. Cause we're their avatars.

SAM

I changed my mind. You can be Sam.

PIG

No, they picked you to be Sam. You have to be Sam. And we have to go to Mount Doom.

SAM

That's stupid.

PIG

Well, that's not a very nice thing to say.

SAM

Sorry. I just think this is a terrible idea.

PIG

Why?

SAM

It makes me feel very worried. That's all.

PIG

I think it sounds awesome!

SAM

That's because your character is silly! You don't take anything seriously!

PIG

Of course I don't! It's a game!

SWAM

It's called Mount Doom. Why would anyone choose to go there?

PIG

It will be an adventure! Imagine the view from the top of the mountain! Come on Sam! Let's go on an adventure! If anything bad happens, I'll save your bacon!

SAM

No.

[*Go to* Level One: Mount Doom *(page 30)*.]

YOU HAVE CHOSEN WHISPERRUN GHOST TOWN

THE MACHINE

You have chosen Whisperrun Ghost Town. Advance Sam and Pig to Whisperrun Ghost Town.

SAM

Wait. What?

PIG

You heard her, let's get going.

SAM

To a ghost town? Um. I didn't pack any sunscreen. My mom says not to go out in the desert without water. Also, there might be rattlesnakes.

PIG

I don't think we have a choice. The players pick and we have to do what they say. Cause we're their avatars.

SAM

I changed my mind. You can be Sam.

PIG

No, they picked you to be Sam. You have to be Sam. And we have to go to Whisperrun Ghost Town.

SAM

That's stupid.

PIG

Well, that's not a very nice thing to say.

SAM

Sorry. I just think this is a terrible idea.

PIG

Why?

SAM

It makes me feel very worried. That's all.

PIG

I think it sounds awesome!

SAM

That's because your character is silly! You don't take anything seriously!

PIG

Of course I don't! It's a game!

SAM

It's a ghost town. Why would anyone choose to go there?

PIG

It will be an adventure! Maybe we'll find a goldmine or treasure! Come on Sam! Let's go on an adventure! If anything bad happens, I'll save your bacon!

SAM

No.

[*Go to* Whisperrun Ghost Town *(page 35).*]

LEVEL ONE

MOUNT DOOM

THE MACHINE

[*Impatiently.*] Sam and Pig arrive at the top of Mount Doom. It is cold, and windy, and steep.

SAM

Wait, what? How did we get here?

PIG

Look at the view! You can see for miles!

SAM

I feel dizzy. I'm going to throw up.

PIG

Look at all the lights out there. The tiny little ant people down below in their tiny little ant cars.

SAM

Don't look down, just don't look down.

PIG

Ha, ha, you're shaking like a leaf.

SAM

I don't like heights.

PIG

[*Pretends to push* SAM.] So what, this scares you?

SAM

WHAT ARE YOU DOING?

PIG

Don't worry. I wasn't actually going to push you.

SAM

I could be killed! What is wrong with you?

PIG

I wasn't actually going to push you! I was just playing!

SAM

That kind of playing isn't funny!

PIG

Let's not leap to any conclusions.

SAM

You're still making a joke!

PIG

Ok, ok. I understand the gravity of the situation. Besides, what happens if you fall off anyway? You just get another life, right?

SAM

I don't know!

PIG

This is just a game, right?

SAM

Not to me!

PIG

If it's a game, there has to be a way to win it, right?

SAM

I don't know.

PIG

Sure. That's how games work.

SAM

How do you win a mountain?

THE MACHINE

Level One: The High Dive Stick Man approaches.

PIG

I don't think the mountain is the bad guy. I think the bad guy is coming now!

[THE MACHINE *has turned into a* HIGH DIVE STICK MAN. *Ominous music.*]

HIGH DIVE STICK MAN (HDSM)

I am the High Dive Stick Man and I am here to issue a challenge. If you jump off the top of Mount Doom with me you'll get a treasure beyond your wildest imagination!

SAM

If I jump off a mountain I will die!

HDSM

No, you'll fly!

PIG

Ooh! We can fly!

SAM

No we can't!

HDSM

Yes, you can! I say you can!

SAM

People can't fly!

PIG

I'm Pig!

SAM

Do you believe every silly thing someone tells you?

PIG

The treasure is right down there! Leap and you'll get it!

SAM

No.

HDSM

Look, I'll make the mountain smaller. The mountain is now half as big!

SAM

I don't care.

HDSM

I'll give you a magic cape!

[*Starts to hand over a cape.*]

SAM

I don't want your stupid cape!

PIG

Never turn down a fashion accessory! I'll take it! I'll leap!

HDSM

You can accompany your friend, but Sam has to leap.

PIG

Leap Sam, leap! I believe in you!

SAM

No, if I jump I'll fall and if I fall I'll crush every bone in my body and it will hurt and my blood will go everywhere and my brains will go splat and and I'll die and then you'll just be a stupid Pig all by yourself and someone will probably kill you and eat you.

PIG

That was mean.

SAM

I'm going to sit here until this game is done.

HDSM

Level ended. Next level begins.

SAM

That's not fair! I didn't even finish this level!

PIG

We didn't get any treasure! I was hoping it was ice cream.

SAM

I don't want to jump off of things or climb things or crawl through things or do any of that stuff.

PIG

But there might be ice cream!

SAM

There also might be death!

PIG

Don't you like ice cream?

SAM

I love ice cream.

THE MACHINE

Next level starting.

[*Go to* Level Two: Battlefield—Sharks or Demon Wolves *(page 40).*]

WHISPERRUN GHOST TOWN

THE MACHINE

[*Impatiently.*] Sam and Pig arrive in Whisperrun Ghost Town. Rotten buildings creak ominously and a tumbleweed rolls across the street. The sound of a coyote howling can be heard in the distance.

SAM

Wait, what? How did we get here?

PIG

Cool! Let's go look in all of the buildings. We can pretend one of them is a saloon and order root beer! [*If the audience equipped* SAM *with a cowboy hat add:* Oh! Your hat is PERFECT for this! *If not, add:* Gee, I wish the players had given you the cowboy hat. Then you'd really be all set for this level.]

SAM

Forget the hat. Those buildings look haunted.

PIG

Root beer floats don't stand a ghost of a chance against me.

SAM

Or at the very least like they'll collapse at any second.

PIG

That one looks like it used to be a jail. We could go play cops and robbers.

SAM

Where is everybody anyway?

PIG

Well, it's a ghost town, so it's probably just us.

SAM

What if something bad happens? There aren't any adults?

PIG

It's fine. Let's go explore.

SAM

What if that thing that just howled comes and tries to eat us?

PIG

I'm sure that was just a sound effect for atmosphere.

SAM

What if it gets dark and it gets cold and we're stuck here? And we die?

PIG

Well, it's a game. If you die, you just get another life, right?

SAM

I don't know!

PIG

This is just a game, right?

SAM

Not to me!

PIG

If it's a game, there has to be a way to win it, right?

SAM

I don't know.

PIG

Sure. That's how games work.

SAM

How do you win a ghost town? I want out of here!

PIG

Ok, we'll just start walking . . . and . . .

SAM

[*Runs to one edge of the stage and encounters an invisible force field.*] OW.

PIG

Well, we won't go that way.

SAM

[*Runs the other way and encounters the force field.*] OW.

PIG

Ok, that way is out too.

SAM

We're trapped in this stupid ghost town like we're in a snow globe!

PIG

Huh.

SAM

We're going to die here!

PIG

I mean, there's nothing to indicate that that's going to happen . . . maybe we need to go into the buildings and find something to move to the next level. Like, solve a puzzle?

SAM

What do you know about anything? You want to play cops and robbers or you want to play saloon or you want to talk about root beer. You don't take anything seriously because you're just an idiot Pig!

PIG

That was mean.

SAM

I'm going to sit here until this game is done.

PIG

I don't think that just sitting there is going to do anything.

SAM

I refuse to play. Playing is stupid. I hate this stupid scary ghost town.

THE MACHINE

Level ended. Next level beginning.

SAM

That's not fair! I didn't even finish this level!

PIG

We didn't go into any of the buildings! We didn't get to look at any of the stuff! I wanted to meet a ghost!

SAM

I don't want to meet a ghost!

PIG

But it might be friendly!

SAM

But it might not!

PIG

But we might find a buried treasure! Like, from an old gold mine!

SAM

Maybe.

PIG

If we can't get out, how could anything get in, anyway?

SAM

I don't know!

PIG

Why be scared of it then?

SAM

I don't know!

THE MACHINE

Next level starting.

[*Go to* Level Two: Battlefield—Sharks or Demon Wolves *(page 40)*.]

LEVEL TWO:
Battlefield—Sharks or Demon Wolves

[Level Two *proceeds directly from either* Mount Doom *or* Whisperrun Ghost Town.]

THE MACHINE

Level Two: Battlefield.

PIG

Battlefield?

SAM

What does battlefield mean?

PIG

Probably that we have to battle something.

SAM

No duh.

PIG

You are very moody.

SAM

I'm sorry! It was in my character description!

PIG

Does that mean you have to behave that way?

SAM

I don't know, you keep making terrible puns. Does that mean you have to behave that way?

PIG

I'm not behaving that way! Those puns are awesome! What do you think we're battling?

SAM

I don't know.

PIG

Which way do you think it's coming from?

SAM

I don't know!

PIG

What do you know?

SAM

That we're not going to have much luck defeating an enemy with a book and a rubber chicken!

PIG

Does the book have anything in it about defeating enemies?

SAM

It's just a book! When I've read stories about defeating enemies the heroes are always really tough, they have super powers or they're super spies, or they have special gear, or lots of training. We're just a kid and a pig. We can't do anything!

PIG

You are very negative.

THE MACHINE

Players: choose the enemy, shark or demon wolf. If you want enemy shark, raise your hand. If you want enemy demon wolf, raise your hand. You have chosen enemy [shark / demon wolf]. [*If the players pick* Shark *say:* "Players, hum this with me!" *(have them hum the* Jaws *theme). If players pick the* Demon Wolf: "Players, add wolf howls for me!"]

SAM

Oh heck no! I'm not fighting either of those things! Both of those things will destroy us!

PIG

No, no, no. You always say that!

SAM

I can't help it!

PIG

If it's a game, there's always a way to win!

SAM

There's no way to win! There's no way and everything is a disaster and I hate everything! And you're not my friend!

PIG

You're not even trying to think of how we could win!

SAM

I can't help it! My brain is stuck on bad things!

PIG

What do you mean?

SAM

I just get stuck! On all the bad thoughts! They rush in and circle around and around and get worse and worse and I can't do what you do!

PIG

What am I doing?

SAM

Trying things! Being cheerful! Not panicking! Asking yourself if something is in the book that we can use?

PIG

Believe me. I'm a pig. I do not want to be eaten by that [demon wolf / shark] but it's right there and it's coming at us and we have to try something because yelling is not going to fix the problem.

SAM

I can't do what you want!

PIG

What?

SAM

I can't calm down and think and be reasonable! My heart is going a million miles an hour and I can't breathe and I think I'm going to die and who cares if that stupid [wolf/shark] eats us? I'm the worst person in the world and I'm stupid and everybody hates me and the players out there are probably really sorry they chose such a useless jerk like me who can't even try to fight the [demon wolf / shark] and we're all going to die anyway!

[SAM *huddles into a ball and starts crying.*]

PIG

Stop the game! Stop the game! Sam is broken! [She/He] can't play the game! Seriously! Stop the game!

THE MACHINE

Uh . . . players, can we pause? Can you yell pause? [*The players yell pause.*] The game is paused.

PIG

Sam, are you ok?

SAM

I can't breathe. I can't breathe.

PIG

Try to calm down. Can you please try to calm down? Imagine that you're blowing bubbles maybe. Breathe in really deeply and then blow out gently so the bubbles don't break.

SAM

I hate this game, I hate this game, I hate this game!

PIG

I'll breathe with you.

SAM

I hate breathing and I'm not going to do it!

PIG

I think you have to breathe. Everybody has to breathe.

SAM

[*Starts laughing in spite of him- or herself.*] Ok fine. I'll breathe.

[*Takes deep calming breaths.*]

PIG

You know, so far, no actual bad thing has happened to us.

SAM

What?

PIG

Well, we were at [Mount Doom / Whisperrun Ghost Town] which seemed scary, but nothing actually happened there, and then we were supposed to fight the [demon wolf / shark] but we didn't have to do that either. Things have seemed scary, but nothing actually has happened.

SAM

Great. That's worse.

PIG

How is that worse?

SAM

Because I look totally stupid freaking out about nothing in front of all the players.

PIG

Everybody has stuff they get scared about.

SAM

I get scared about everything.

PIG

It's not your fault. They designed it in your character. Just like they designed me to be terribly good looking.

SAM

For a pig.

PIG

For an anything.

SAM

My brain really does just get stuck on all the bad things that could happen and my heart gets going really fast and it's like there's a tornado inside my head and I can't think at all and I know I'm saying mean things to you and I don't mean to but I can't seem to help it.

PIG

You can't just think about good thoughts? That's what I do.

SAM

No, I don't think so. I don't think that's the way I work. 'Cause of the anxiety. The voice said I had anxiety. I don't think you can just think your way out of anxiety.

PIG

Oh. What can you do?

SAM

I'm not sure.

PIG

Well, we're going to have to figure something out if we want to help the players win the game.

SAM

I know.

PIG

Every level has been something that you're scared of. What else are you scared of?

SAM

I am scared of eleven things in order of least to most scary: heights, ghost towns, sharks, demon wolves, roller coasters, vampire bats, the abyss, a zombie apocalypse, the dark, car accidents, and something happening to my mom or dad.

PIG

Woah.

SAM

I told you my brain is full of scary things.

PIG

Well, up next will be roller coasters or vampire bats?

SAM

The thing is, I think roller coasters look like fun. But I'm too scared to go on them. I think a lot of things look like fun. I even think maybe playing this game could be fun now that it's on pause and we don't actually have to do it. Like, when I read about things in books, adventures and things, they sound like fun. But in real life my body gets all sick and I can't go do it. Like talking to other people. I haven't been nice to you at all Pig. If you didn't have to be my friend because of this game, you wouldn't be either. And I don't want to be mean to you, I just get really stressed out and then I start yelling. When I calm down I know it's not nice but I'm not sure how to fix it.

PIG

Anxiety seems hard. I wonder why the game gave you that attribute and didn't make you totally awesome like me?

SAM

I don't know, why don't you ask it?

THE MACHINE

Next level starting. Roller coaster option denied.

[*Go to* Level Three: Vampire Bats *(page 48)*.]

LEVEL THREE: Vampire Bats

[*Continues on from* Level Two. SAM *and* PIG *hand the narrator four cards with the possible answers on them. Note: The dialogue in this section takes a lot of different directions because the audience can choose what the characters say. Players must choose* Why Does Sam Have Anxiety *and* How Can Sam Overcome Anxiety *(in either order) before* Battle Vampire Bats *to get to winning scenario. Until they do that, the avatars die and respawn. Too many deaths and* THE MACHINE *locks them out and the game goes on autopilot for a time.*]

PIG

Hey wait, hey wait! We're not ready to start the next level yet! We want to ask you some questions!

THE MACHINE

You are in a dark cave. There is barely any light and the sound of water drips. You smell a strange and funny smell and hear the rustling of a lot of wings. Suddenly, something flies near Sam's hair.

SAM

[*Pantomimes reacting to a bat flying near* [*his/her*] *head.*] Eww! What was that?

PIG

No wait. We need some answers. Hey. Hey you! We have some questions!

SAM

I don't know Pig, maybe we just need to get out of here. I don't like the dark.

PIG

No. I want to know why the game made you like this and how we help you win. HEY, HEY YOU MACHINE! WE NEED SOME ANSWERS.

THE MACHINE

Fine. [*To the players.*] You are in a dark cave with no light that is filled with vampire bats. You have a limited time before they attack you and suck your blood. I will read you some possible questions. The second time through I will read them and you can vote for which one you want to choose. You can ask: A) Why does Sam have anxiety? B) How can Sam overcome anxiety? or C) Why is a raven like a writing desk? If you want to ask The Machine A) Why does Sam have anxiety, raise your hand. B) How can Sam overcome anxiety, raise your hand. C) Why is a raven like a writing desk, raise your hand.

[*If audience chooses* A, *go to* Why Does Sam Have Anxiety *(page 50); if audience chooses* B, *go to* How Can Sam Overcome Anxiety *(page 51); if audience chooses* C, *go to* Why Is a Raven Like a Writing Desk *(page 52)*.]

WHY DOES SAM HAVE ANXIETY

THE MACHINE

Sam has anxiety because that's the way Sam's character was designed. Just like you were designed to be a pig. Some avatars are designed with brown skin, and some with black hair, and some are tall, and some are short. Some can run and some are in wheelchairs. Some avatars are neurotypical, and some have attributes like anxiety that make the game more challenging for them. They can still win the game, but they have to learn how to play differently.

SAM

I can still win?

PIG

Of course you can.

SAM

Oh.

PIG

Unless you give up and don't try.

SAM

But it's hard.

THE MACHINE

Yes. It is a challenge. But that is why I gave you Pig to help you. [*To the players.*] Players, if you want to ask The Machine: A) How can Sam overcome anxiety, raise your hand. B) Why is a raven like a writing desk, raise your hand. C) No more questions, fight vampire bats.

[*Go to appropriate section; if audience chooses* C, *go to* Battle Vampire Bats WITHOUT How to Defeat Anxiety *(page 54).*]

HOW CAN SAM OVERCOME ANXIETY

THE MACHINE

Sam can overcome [her/his] anxiety by learning new patterns of thinking. [She/He] can use the breathing idea that you gave [her/him] before, where [she/he] breathes in and out slowly to calm [her/his] body. When your body gets really upset, it convinces your mind that there is something to be afraid of, even if there really isn't. If [her/his] anxiety gets too bad, [she/he] can go with [her/his] parents to talk to a doctor and they can make a plan to help [her/him]. [*To the players.*] If you want to ask The Machine A) Why does Sam have anxiety, raise your hand. B) Why is a raven like a writing desk, raise your hand. C) No more questions—fight vampire bats!

> [*Go to appropriate section; if audience has already chosen* Why *and* How, *and now chooses* C, *go to* Battle Vampire Bats WITH How to Defeat Anxiety *(page 57).*]

WHY IS A RAVEN LIKE A WRITING DESK

[*Note, the players might choose this scene repeatedly. Do it just the same twice, but the third time* THE MACHINE *should use the* "You have temporarily been locked out and the game is on autopilot" *command to get things back on track.*]

THE MACHINE

Players, why are you asking me silly riddles in a time like this? While you waste time, Vampire Bats attack and kill Sam and Pig.

SAM

Wait, what?

PIG

Oh no!

SAM

Ow! Ow! They're so bitey! Stop it!

PIG

I'm too pretty to die so young!

SAM

I'm dying . . . I'm dying . . .

PIG

Now I'll become an angel and you'll finally see pigs fly.

[SAM *and* PIG *die. They have no memory of this when they respawn.*]

THE MACHINE

Respawn from last set point. [SAM *and* PIG *stand back up.*]

[*To the players.*] You are in a dark cave with no light that is filled with vampire bats. You have a limited time before they attack you and suck your blood. If you want to ask The Machine A) Why does Sam have anxiety, raise your hand. B) How can Sam overcome anxiety, raise your hand. C) Why is a raven like a writing desk, raise your hand. D) No more questions—fight vampire bats!

[*Go to appropriate section.*]

BATTLE THE VAMPIRE BATS WITHOUT HOW TO DEFEAT ANXIETY

PIG

Ok, so you have anxiety because you have anxiety, and now we're going to battle some vampire bats.

SAM

But we don't know how to make the anxiety go away! They didn't ask how to make the anxiety go away!

PIG

Oh yeah.

SAM

Why didn't they ask that?

PIG

I don't know? Are you going to break again? And have a meltdown? Vampire bats suck people's blood right? So this is going to be bad?

SAM

Actually, I think I read in a book that they mostly feed on livestock.

PIG

Livestock?

SAM

Like . . . pigs?

PIG

Oh no. Oh no, no, no, no. DO SOMETHING.

SAM

I don't know how! I don't know how! They didn't ask how!

THE MACHINE

The vampire bats begin to approach.

PIG

I'm not livestock! I'm basically a person . . . 'cause I can talk and make jokes and I'm so cute . . . I'm, what's that word?

SAM

Anthropomorphic?

PIG

What?

SAM

It's the word for when movies and books and plays make animals act like people.

PIG

You know all of these big words but what use are they now! Oh bats! Hear me! Take this RUBBER CHICKEN INSTEAD!

THE MACHINE

The bats are not interested in the chicken. Vampire Bats attack and kill Sam and Pig.

SAM

Wait, what?

PIG

Oh no!

SAM

Ow! Ow! They're so bitey! Stop it!

PIG

I'm too pretty to die so young!

SAM

I'm dying . . . I'm dying . . .

PIG

Now I'll become and angel and you'll finally see pigs fly.

[SAM *and* PIG *die. They have no memory of this when they respawn.*]

THE MACHINE

Respawn from last set point. [*To the players.*] You are in a dark cave with no light that is filled with vampire bats. You have a limited time before they attack you and suck your blood. If you want to ask The Machine: A) How can Sam overcome anxiety, raise your hand. B) Why is a raven like a writing desk, raise your hand.

[*Go to appropriate section.*]

BATTLE THE VAMPIRE BATS WITH HOW TO DEFEAT ANXIETY

PIG

Ok. Well, we don't have time for you to go to the doctor right now, so you just have to breathe and try to change your pattern of thinking on your own.

SAM

What? How?

PIG

Uh. Here. Squeeze this rubber chicken when you get anxious. It will give your brain something else to do.

SAM

Um. Ok?

PIG

Now. What do you know about vampire bats? Is there something in that book?

SAM

Vampire bats feed mostly on livestock?

PIG

What? What's a livestock?

SAM

You know, not people like they do in books like Dracula. But like, cows, and pigs . . .

PIG

WHAT????

SAM

Oh . . . dear.

PIG

Save me, save me, save me.

SAM

This is a lot of pressure!

PIG

Squeeze the chicken! Squeeze the chicken, do your breathing, and use your big brain and save me!

SAM

Um . . . uh . . . ok. What don't bats like?

PIG

Garlic? I can eat garlic?

SAM

That's just in movies! Also we don't have garlic!

PIG

I don't know!

SAM

Light! They don't like light! Run this way and we'll try to get out of the cave and away from the bats! If we come out into the light they'll go away!

[PIG *and* SAM *run around and around on stage ducking from imaginary bats but there's no escaping them.*]

PIG

Where is the end to this cave? I am too tired for this!

SAM

I don't know! This is stupid! I'm trying and I still can't win!

THE MACHINE

You did not defeat the vampire bats. Next level. Zombie Apocalypse.

LEVEL FOUR: Zombie Thoughts

SAM

You have GOT to be kidding me!

THE MACHINE

You are on a barren wasteland. There are no rocks, or trees, or plants, or buildings. You hear moaning and shuffling in the distance. The zombies approach in three minutes.

PIG

Do zombies prefer people or livestock?

SAM

Every level is scarier and worse than the thing before! I said all of the things I was scared of and the game is just making all of them happen! We haven't won a single level yet!

PIG

I don't want to be killed and eaten by zombies. I don't want to be a zombie pig. I have so many plans. I was going to go to college. Get a degree in mathematics. Invent a new kind of pi. Invent a new kind of pie. Calculate that pie with pi and eat the pi pie.

SAM

We have absolutely nothing to fight zombies with. Nothing. We have a book and a chicken. Wait. Where's the book?

PIG

I think you dropped it when I gave you the chicken.

SAM

We have a rubber chicken. You need stuff to fight zombies with! Like, weapons and a fort and things! Breathing is not going to help us fight zombies! I hate this game and I hate anxiety and I hate you Pig and I hate my life and I hate breathing and I hate . . .

PIG

Woah. Woah. Wait.

SAM

I quit! I quit this game! I quit it, I quit it! I quit it!

PIG

You can't quit!

SAM

Why not?

PIG

Because it doesn't work like that! The players can quit the game but this is our life! We're in the game until the end!

SAM

Well, that's stupid.

PIG

You say that a lot! Everything is stupid! But the voice said that that was your anxiety talking and that you have to learn to think differently and not give up if you don't want your anxiety to beat you.

SAM

I just want to be a normal kid! With no anxiety! I just want to go back to the beginning and have them pick a different avatar who is less stupid!

PIG

You're not stupid Sam! You're just you. Everybody has something that makes the game harder for them. I mean. I have hooves! It is very hard to hold things when you have hooves! Everybody feels stupid sometimes. Everybody messes up and loses sometimes.

SAM

I've lost every single level so far!

PIG

But you don't lose for real unless you give up. There has to be some way to win this game, right? I mean, whoever heard of a game where there was no way to win? And you're only scared of eleven things, right? Maybe we just have to survive the eleven things and we win.

SAM

Eleven things! That's WAY too many.

PIG

What were they again?

SAM

Heights, ghost towns, sharks, demon wolves, roller coasters, vampire bats, the abyss, a zombie apocalypse, the dark, car accidents, and something happening to my mom or dad.

PIG

It's a game. We have to think our way through. Even though we keep losing, we're still making progress through the levels!

SAM

Think. We have to think. Ok. Deep breaths. Deep breaths. Thinking. Wait. We're still making progress?

PIG

Yes. The machine keeps moving us to a higher level!

SAM

But we keep losing.

PIG

Maybe you shouldn't get hamstrung about that.

SAM

So we're not really losing? Huh. So what if we're wrong about who we're fighting?

PIG

I don't understand. Zombies is the next thing on your list, right?

SAM

But . . . zombies aren't real. I read about them in books and I see them in movies but zombies aren't real.

PIG

Do you think they could be true?

SAM

No. I'm scared of them, but I know they're not real. The things I'm scared of: ghosts, demon wolves, sharks attacking me when I'm in a swimming pool, most of that stuff can't really happen and I know that when I'm thinking straight. I do. But I'm scared anyway.

PIG

Ok.

SAM

But my brain just keeps having scary thoughts and acting without thinking, like I'm a zombie. Maybe the zombies we're fighting aren't real zombies coming to eat us but the zombie thoughts that make me afraid of things for no reason.

PIG

I like this idea a lot better, because I don't think thoughts like to eat pigs.

SAM

Maybe what I have to do is think about whether or not something is really real and really going to hurt me or whether my anxiety is making me dream up this scary thing and be afraid for no good reason.

PIG

We haven't actually had to fight anything for real, have we?

SAM

No, we haven't. The Machine keeps saying we'll have to, but nothing ever actually happens to us.

PIG

Although, I did have the funniest feeling of déjà vu, like I might have had other lives once.

SAM

So I think the zombies aren't actual zombies but zombie THOUGHTS. And if I tell the zombie thoughts to just STOP. If I stop and think about whether or not something can actually happen or if it's just my anxiety talking, maybe I can win?

PIG

Well, try it. What's the worst that can happen if you're wrong?

SAM

We get slaughtered and eaten by a hoard of zombies?

PIG

Well, sure, but that would happen either way, right?

SAM

Ok, hey! You! You up there! There are no such thing as zombies and they cannot hurt us! So we're going to . . . sit here and . . . sing "The Song That Never Ends" until you let us win this level or the zombies eat us. Whichever happens first.

[SAM *and* PIG *sing "The Song That Never Ends."*]

THE MACHINE

Oh stop, stop, stop. Fine. Level defeated.

LEVELING UP

PIG

We did it Sam! We won the level! We won!

SAM

Using the power of being super annoying!

PIG

I didn't even know we had that power!

SAM

Oh yeah. Any time I want to bother my parents I just sing that at them. It also works to talk to my mom a lot about *Minecraft*.

PIG

Great. So now your anxiety is fixed forever.

SAM

I don't think so Pig. I mean, The Machine said it was just a part of me.

PIG

Like my adorable pink nose is a part of me.

SAM

Yeah. And we haven't even dealt with my worst fears yet, like car accidents or something bad happening to my mom and dad. And that's not like zombies. I've been in a car accident and it was super scary so I know it can really happen.

PIG

So what do we do?

SAM

I can maybe deal with some of the zombie thought anxieties. But I don't think the bigger ones are something you or even the players can help me with. I think this is something I have to get a grown up to help me with.

THE MACHINE

Sam has LEVELED UP.

SAM

Oh hey cool!

THE MACHINE

Sam has gained 50XP and new equipment: the Copper Mind Shield.

[*Sam puts on the copper mind-shield hat.*]

PIG

What do I get? Do I get something?

THE MACHINE

Pig gets a sandwich.

PIG

YES!

SAM

What can I get with my XP?

THE MACHINE

You can purchase character customizations including The Bubble Machine of Awesomeness, The Tangle Band of Pacification, or The Stuffed Hedgehog Named Henry.

SAM

Players, which should I choose? Should I choose The Bubble Machine of Awesomeness? The Tangle Band of Pacification? Or The Stuffed Hedgehog Named Henry? [*Audience chooses* Bubbles, Tangle Band, *or* Henry.] What do I do with this?? This seems even less useful than a book!

PIG

I'm just glad it's not a real hedgehog because there's only room around here for one cute talking animal.

THE MACHINE

Sam and Pig will now face the EVIL ABYSS on DIFFICULTY LEVEL SEVEN.

PIG

Wait, what?

SAM

No, no, no . . . level down! Sam will level down! I will give this [bubble machine / tangle band / hedgehog] back!

PIG

Here we go again . . .

BOSS BATTLE: The Evil Abyss

THE MACHINE

Sam and Pig are in the evil abyss. There is no light. There is no sound. There is no way out.

PIG

Luckily, pigs are VERY good at seeing in the dark.

SAM

Is that true?

PIG

Yes, I can see you clear as day just on my right.

SAM

[*Reaches out a hand and smacks* PIG.]

PIG

OH MY GOSH. WHAT WAS THAT?

SAM

That was me!

PIG

How did you get to my left so fast?

SAM

I haven't moved. You can't see a thing.

PIG

Well, whatever.

[*Crunch noise.*]

SAM

What was that?

PIG

I'm just finishing up my sandwich before we have to battle anything. I would hate to drop it. It's a very good sandwich.

SAM

You ate it? What if we needed it to win this level?

PIG

Uh. Huh. That did not occur to me.

SAM

Just don't make any more freaky noises, ok? I can't see anything and this is scary enough.

PIG

Fine. I'll just go stand over here . . .

SAM

Wait, don't go anywhere! You can't actually see anything!

PIG

I'm just going a few feet . . .

[PIG*'s voice abruptly dies out.*]

SAM

Pig? Pig? Pig WHERE ARE YOU?

[THE MACHINE *puts on a mask and turns into the* GOBLIN VOICE.]

GOBLIN VOICE

[*Whispers.*] Sam.

SAM

Is that you Pig?

GOBLIN VOICE

No Sam. It's me.

SAM

Pig, if you're playing a trick on me. I don't think it's funny. I will throw [bubble machine / tangle band / Henry] at you.

GOBLIN VOICE

Why do you keep calling me a pig, Sam? That's not very nice.

SAM

Mom?

GOBLIN VOICE

It's not very nice to call people pigs at all!

SAM

Is that really you Mom?

GOBLIN VOICE

I am so disappointed in you. I raised you to be better than this. You've hurt my feelings now.

SAM

I'm sorry Mom! I was just talking to my friend Pig.

GOBLIN VOICE

You don't have any friends. Quit lying to me.

SAM

I'm sorry I hurt your feelings, but why are you being this way? You always tell me to use my words nicely.

GOBLIN VOICE

Because you should know the truth. I'm disappointed in you.

SAM

Mom, come here please? It's dark and I'm alone and scared, and I do have a friend named Pig.

GOBLIN VOICE

No. I won't come.

SAM

Please?

GOBLIN VOICE

No. I don't want to be with you.

SAM

Where's Dad?

GOBLIN VOICE

He's playing golf.

SAM

Wait, what?

GOBLIN VOICE

Sorry. He's playing . . .

SAM

Hockey?

GOBLIN VOICE

Yes. Hockey.

SAM

Something's funny.

GOBLIN VOICE

It's sure not you. You are never funny.

SAM

I don't think you're really my mom. Now that I have this copper mind shield, it's helping me stop and think about things and I think you're not my mom.

GOBLIN VOICE

I am too your mom.

SAM

My dad would never play golf.

GOBLIN VOICE

Now that we got rid of you, he has a lot more time for hobbies.

SAM

That's mean. Also, Dad thinks golf is super boring. He would never do that.

GOBLIN VOICE

Don't disrespect me Sam!

SAM

You're pretend! You're pretending to be my mom!

GOBLIN VOICE

Come over here Sam and see if I'm your mom or not!

SAM

[*Takes a step toward the voice.*]

GOBLIN VOICE

Yes. Come here. Come to your mother.

SAM

Ok. You are definitely not my mother. My mother never calls herself mother! And my father would not play golf! This is a trap!

GOBLIN VOICE

Fine. See my real face.

[THE MACHINE *as* GOBLIN VOICE *emerges. It is wearing a hideous goblin mask. It is very scary.*]

SAM

What did you do with Pig? I really need Pig right now.

GOBLIN VOICE

Pig is gone. It's just you and me now.

SAM

[*Looks at* bubble machine / tangle band / Henry *in hand.*] I do not think throwing this at you would help.

GOBLIN VOICE

No. That would be useless. Like you. Sam, your parents were in a car accident. It's just me now.

SAM

What? Are they ok . . . are they in the hospital? Wait. Deep breaths Sam. This thing is probably lying to you.

GOBLIN VOICE

I'm not lying. Do you want to see pictures? Here, let me send you a vision!

SAM

[*The* GOBLIN VOICE *is in* [*her/his*]*head.*] What? I don't like imagining this. The copper shield should protect me from this.

GOBLIN VOICE

Sam, it's only a copper mind shield. It's not gold, or diamond. And you wasted your XP on . . . that.

SAM

[*Looks at* bubble machine / tangle band / Henry *in* [*her/his*] *hand.*] You're lying. You're a demon. Demons lie.

GOBLIN VOICE

Can't you see them? Your parents, bruised and broken?

SAM

Yes. It's in my head. The bad pictures are swirling around.

GOBLIN VOICE

Also, Pig, your only friend, left because [she/he] was so tired of you. Your whining, and complaining, and saying no all the time. Pig wants a friend who wants to have adventures!

SAM

No! Pig left because I asked [her/him] to crunch the sandwich less loudly! [She/He] was being polite! You should be polite!

GOBLIN VOICE

No, it was because of you!

SAM

No. Wait. You know the thing I'm most scared of is something happening to my parents. And now you're telling me that happened?

GOBLIN VOICE

You MADE it happen! By being you!

SAM

Wait. You can't make a car accident happen with your mind.

GOBLIN VOICE

Are you sure Sam?

SAM

You're lying to me!

GOBLIN VOICE

You can see them Sam! You know it's true!

SAM

No. Wait. I'm imagining them. Like the zombies. It's different. I can't see anything. It's an abyss. You're combining all of the things I'm scared of. That's not fair!

GOBLIN VOICE

Life's not fair, Sam! You're imagining them then, in your head, and that's good enough for me! As long as you're busy imagining bad things, you can't do anything else and I win!

SAM

[*Looks at* bubble machine / tangle band / Henry *in hand.*] This thing has to be good for something.

GOBLIN VOICE

Picture it Sam . . . no more hugs, no more I love yous, where will you go? Who will take care of you?

SAM

[*Plays with* bubble machine / tangle band / Henry *in hand.*] I DON'T WANT TO PICTURE THAT! I'll just . . . focus on this [bubble machine / tangle band / hedgehog]. They are . . . kinda soothing, I guess.

GOBLIN VOICE

I didn't want to have to do this Sam!

SAM

Do what?

GOBLIN VOICE

Send you another bad vision! This one will be EVEN WORSE! It will be . . .

SAM

But they're visions right? So . . . they're not really happening.

GOBLIN VOICE

I . . . Uh . . . No! They're real!

SAM

So I'm going to keep focusing on this thing and . . . try to think of happy thoughts instead.

GOBLIN VOICE

People really die in car accidents! You said it yourself!

SAM

Yes, but I don't think they did right now. I think you're lying. I think I'm imagining. My brain does that. It imagines terrible things. I don't know why, that's just the way it works and that's ok. But I don't have to let my brain OR YOU win. And if they did die, I would feel really sad. But imagining it now doesn't really help me. Feeling sad about something that hasn't really happened doesn't really help me.

GOBLIN VOICE

There is no helping you! You are alone!

SAM

I'm going to play with this toy and I'm going to imagine what Pig would do. I'm going to imagine Pig telling me a bad joke. And we're eating sandwiches. [*Whisperrun Ghost Town option:* And we're going to explore the ghost town this time because I know nothing's there to hurt me. And we find a buried treasure!][*Mount Doom option:* And we're at the top of Mount Doom and I'm super brave and I take the challenge and we have a treasure beyond our imagination! Which, knowing Pig, is just a bunch of food.]

GOBLIN VOICE

That isn't true! You were a coward there!

SAM

But this isn't true either! And I prefer to think the good thoughts! Not the zombie ones!

GOBLIN VOICE

What can I say to scare you?

SAM

I'm not going to answer that! I'm just going to keep playing with this! And I'm going to ignore you!

GOBLIN VOICE

You're stupid! Everyone hates you! You'll fail school and never amount to anything! Your brain is all messed up and you can never succeed! You're not listening to me!!!

[SAM *plays with toy.*]

SAM

I'm thinking about . . . vacation. And I'm going on a roller coaster and I'm brave. And reading a funny book. And then I'm eating pizza! It's pizza and movie night with Mom and Dad! I am taking deep breaths. The scary thoughts are there but that's ok. I am the boss of my brain. It is not the boss of me. I am the boss of my brain. It is not the boss of me. I am the boss of my brain. It is not the boss of me.

GOBLIN VOICE

Fine. I give up. You win this time Sam.

SAM

I do? I defeated the final boss battle? All by myself?

GOBLIN VOICE

No. Are you kidding me? I'll be here forever. I'm just going away for now.

SAM

What?

GOBLIN VOICE

Bye Sam.

SAM

Do I get more XP or anything? A better mind shield? A sword? I'd like a sword.

GOBLIN VOICE

Those tools gave you a beginning to a way to withstand me. Everything else is up to you.

SAM

Can I at least have Pig back?

GOBLIN VOICE

Fine.

SAM

Pig? Pig???

PIG

You did it Sam! I could see you talking to someone but it was like I was trapped in a plastic box and couldn't get out to help you!

SAM

That sounds scary!

PIG

Nah, it was fine. I just used the time to practice my mime skills and to sing "The Song That Never Ends" as loudly as I wanted. Cause nobody could be annoyed. And I knew you would get me out eventually.

SAM

How did you know that?

PIG

Because I have faith in you, Sam. You are stronger than you know.

SAM

I wish I believed in me that much.

PIG

Well, I think it's all a matter of practice. Everybody gets scared sometimes. Whether they have anxiety or not. Even me. But I'm just better at dealing with it, I think. Ready for the next level?

SAM

How many levels are there?

PIG

I think it's infinite.

SAM

You can't win?

PIG

Nah. But if you try, I think maybe we can have more fun while we're doing it.

BALLET FOR ALIENS

by Gerard Hernandez, Oliver Kokai-Means, and Jennifer A. Kokai

ORIGINAL COMMISSIONED PRODUCTION HISTORY

Commissioned by Plan-B Theatre for their 2023 school year tour

Originally featuring two casts: Tamari Dunbar & Amona Faatau and Danny Borba & Estephani Cerros

Costume and Prop Design by Arika Schockmel

Tour Manager, Kallie Filanda

Directed by Jerry Rapier

CHARACTERS

Jacob Twelve years old. Suffers from chronic health issues. Likes turkey sandwiches, orange blankets, ballet, and *Minecraft*. Hates nurses who are bad at putting in IVs.

Sophie Probably mid-twenties. As far as Jacob is concerned, she's an adult but not like, a MOM-aged adult. A nurse. Or possibly an alien.

[On stage: A chair, a machine with many buttons and dials. The machine is probably cardboard. JACOB, *twelve, is in the chair. He is very, very nervous. He looks like he might cry. But he's very quiet.* SOPHIE, *his nurse, talks to him.]*

JACOB

This is my second time.

SOPHIE

Ok, so you know the procedure.

JACOB

Is it the same as last time? The exact same?

SOPHIE

Well, I wasn't your nurse last time, but yes, it should be the same thing.

JACOB

No thank you.

SOPHIE

No thank you?

JACOB

I know that everyone says this will help me. To get the infusion. But the nurse last time poked me FOUR times to put the needle in and it really hurt and no thank you.

SOPHIE

I'm pretty good at putting needles in.

JACOB

How good?

SOPHIE

Good. Anyway, you know you need the infusion to feel better.

JACOB

I know.

SOPHIE

So you only found out recently why you were sick, huh?

JACOB

Yes.

SOPHIE

That must have been a big deal.

JACOB

I had to go to a hospital really far away. For tests and things. It was really scary.

SOPHIE

Is it a relief now? That you know what's wrong?

JACOB

No. It's weird to have a disease that makes your stomach feel weird and light and makes you spend so much time in the bathroom. And when I have a flare, which is what my doctor calls it when I feel really, really bad, it gets in the way of everything. Like, I haven't been able to go to ballet for weeks.

SOPHIE

You do ballet?

JACOB

Yep.

SOPHIE

I used to do ballet too. I even studied it in college.

JACOB

You're a nurse, shouldn't you have studied nursing in college?

SOPHIE

I was a double major. You can study more than one thing in college.

JACOB

Ok, but I hope you MOSTLY studied nursing.

SOPHIE

I studied enough to know all about your disease.

JACOB

Oh, there's nothing wrong with ME medically.

SOPHIE

But we were just talking about your diagnosis . . .

JACOB

Ok, so the doctors did tell me I have a disease but that was all just a story. The real truth is it's because my parents are aliens and I'm an alien too.

SOPHIE

Really?

JACOB

Yes.

SOPHIE

You're an alien?

JACOB

I've thought about this a lot, since I first got sick. Because I didn't know why I was sick and I thought I might die. And then when I found out I had Crohn's disease, which you can't even TALK about in polite conversation because bowels, I decided that was a made-up disease and the trouble is really with earth food.

SOPHIE

Earth food?

JACOB

And earth oxygen. And earth bathrooms. Everything earth. I have proof.

SOPHIE

You have proof you're an alien?

JACOB

Yes. My house has caught fire four times.

SOPHIE

Your house caught fire FOUR TIMES?

JACOB

Yes.

SOPHIE

Ok, so that's very unfortunate, but how is that proof?

JACOB

So I wasn't home any of the times. And my mom claims that every time she was cooking something and caught the kitchen on fire. But I never saw any evidence with my own eyes.

SOPHIE

Ok?

JACOB

So I have another theory. There was never any kitchen fires. They've hidden our space ship in the garage.

SOPHIE

Have you ever seen a space ship in your garage?

JACOB

No, because it's HIDDEN. Our garage is full of boxes and we never clean it.

SOPHIE

Ok. So let's accept that there's a hidden spaceship in your garage. What does that have to do with kitchen fires?

JACOB

They WEREN'T kitchen fires, they were caused by working on repairing the space ship. The garage is next to the kitchen. And they were . . . working on the fuel system or using a blow torch and they caught the whole thing on fire. It's hard to repair a space ship. That's why it's taking so long.

SOPHIE

That explains why you're sick?

JACOB

Yes. My parents are aliens. They crash landed here. It's not impossible for us to survive here, but there's something in Earth food that's toxic and over time it made me sick. They told me you can't catch Crohn's disease, but I had to get it somehow. It must be like radiation, you know. They say radiation makes you a superhero but really it just slowly kills you.

SOPHIE

I see. But you're not dying. I know we don't have a cure. But we have treatments that will make you ok.

JACOB

I'm not sure.

SOPHIE

I promise. You're not. Especially if you get the treatments.

JACOB

The needles hurt and it is scary and I just want my mom to fix the spaceship.

SOPHIE

I understand, but I can't help with that. But I can help you get through the treatment.

JACOB

Unless my PARENTS aren't the aliens, YOU'RE the aliens and you're experimenting on me.

SOPHIE

I'm not an alien.

JACOB

Of course you'd say that.

SOPHIE

I was born in Ogden.

JACOB

So you've done your research on local cities, alien.

SOPHIE

Fine. You've caught me.

JACOB

I have?

SOPHIE

That's right humanoid. My name is really Xenu 16 and I am from Mars. I was sent here to gather information on human boys and I selected you as my test subject.

JACOB

I knew it.

SOPHIE

We do not understand why human boys do what human boys do. They do many strange things. For example, we have observed they play simulation games where they do things for pretend on a computer. What is the purpose of these games?

JACOB

They're fun?

SOPHIE

Why do human boys make such a big mess?

JACOB

We don't all make big messes.

SOPHIE

We have observed this to be generally true, however.

JACOB

How does doing medical experiments on me help you solve this?

SOPHIE

We have . . . I am not sure.

JACOB

Uh huh.

SOPHIE

We have heard you say that you do ballet. We do not understand ballet. We want to know how to get good at ballet and so we will experiment on you.

JACOB

What if instead of making me sick I just did ballet for you?

SOPHIE

Aliens do not learn from observation, they learn from abducting people and experimenting on them. Everybody knows that.

JACOB

Aliens are bad scientists then.

SOPHIE

Maybe.

JACOB

You're a weird nurse. I've never had a nurse pretend to be an alien before.

SOPHIE

I am not pretending.

JACOB

Why do you look just like a human then?

SOPHIE

Advanced technology.

JACOB

If you have technology so advanced you can change your face, why do you need to hook me up to a machine every month for an entire day? Why can't you just . . . wave something over me? Or rearrange my molecules?

SOPHIE

[*She is* SOPHIE *again.*] You've got me there. I don't know. I wish we could.

JACOB

Me too.

SOPHIE

You have a big imagination.

JACOB

I don't really think I do. I'm just stalling so you don't stab me. I don't really believe you're an alien.

SOPHIE

For right now, whether someone is an alien or not, we need to get you the medicine that helps you survive on earth.

JACOB

Ok.

SOPHIE

But let's keep pretending.

JACOB

Grown-ups don't pretend.

SOPHIE

Grown-ups pretend all the time. But they keep it a secret. They pretend they're confident when they're scared. They pretend they're successful when they're struggling. They pretend Halloween is for the kids and then they eat all the best candy while you're sleeping.

JACOB

That's what my dad does, because I can't eat it. I blame it on the sugar monster.

SOPHIE

See, imagination? Let's see what's on TV. You can watch TV and pretend it's not happening.

JACOB

It takes all day. That's a LOT of pretending.

SOPHIE

I know. But what does it hurt to try? [*She turns on an imaginary TV. She changes the channels.*] Wow. There's really nothing on, but this little kid's show, *Explora* something.

JACOB

Oh, the Explorer show. I used to watch that show all the time when I was younger. My favorite character was her friend the lemur.

SOPHIE

So should I leave it on?

JACOB

It's better than nothing.

SOPHIE

While I make some notes about your medical history you can watch the show. Try not to worry.

JACOB

Try not to worry about big, fat needles? Or that super painful stuff that is supposed to numb you but actually hurts really bad itself? Try not to worry. Ha.

[JACOB *imagines.* SOPHIE *turns into Explora the Explorer. It's a parody so it's fair use. She has a backpack, takes out a lemur puppet, puts it on. She turns to* JACOB. *She speaks in an exaggerated voice through this whole section.*]

SOPHIE

Hola, amigos. Today we're going to help our friend Jacob.

JACOB

WHAT is happening?

SOPHIE

We're going to use the magic map to find three things that will make Jacob happy while he gets his infusion.

JACOB

Sophie?

SOPHIE

Silly, that's not my name. My name is Explora.

JACOB

Ok, one of us has lost our minds.

SOPHIE

We definitely haven't because we're USING OUR imaginations. And they live IN our minds. Just imagine, Jacob!

JACOB

I think I liked it better when you were an alien? Your voice is . . . very high and squeaky now.

SOPHIE

It's ENTHUSIASM, Jacob. Explora is just very, very, very enthusiastic.

JACOB

I'm not really sure what you want me to do here.

SOPHIE

Well, what does it look like in our world?

JACOB

The walls are this like, light green color, and it's kind of cold, and we're in a room with just a chair and a big beeping machine?

SOPHIE

We can be anywhere in our imagination and that doesn't sound like fun.

JACOB

No kidding.

SOPHIE

If you can believe your parents are aliens, I bet you can believe you're in a cartoon kids' show. I dare you.

JACOB

Fine. It's bright and colorful and super simple because they're background images and things only appear when you talk about them.

SOPHIE

So what are we looking for on our magic map?

JACOB

I don't know.

SOPHIE

What will help you feel calm and safe?

JACOB

My orange blanket?

SOPHIE

Ok. We need three things though!

JACOB

Are you serious?

SOPHIE

Three things!

JACOB

OK fine. My orange blanket and . . . a turkey sandwich.

SOPHIE

That's two!

JACOB

I don't know . . . you could give me the TV remote and I could try to find something else to watch while we do this? Because this is super cringey.

SOPHIE

Where IS the TV remote?

JACOB

You JUST had it. Wait. Where is my orange blanket?

SOPHIE

It's missing! I bet Stabber took it!

JACOB

Stabber?

SOPHIE

Oh yes. He's a penguin who takes things and also he tries to put in IVs and doesn't succeed on the first try.

JACOB

Oh. I hate Stabber.

SOPHIE

Everyone hates Stabber.

JACOB

Ok. How do we find these things? I don't even really remember this show super well.

SOPHIE

Well, we look on the magic map and three blankets will appear and I'll ask you to point to the orange one . . .

JACOB

Which I will do like, super easily because I'm twelve and this show is for babies?

SOPHIE

My friend Jacob is VERY grouchy, kids. Point to the person on stage who is VERY grouchy.

JACOB

WHO ARE YOU TALKING TO?

SOPHIE

That's right! Jacob is the grouchy kid!

JACOB

No one is pointing at me! Nobody better be pointing at me. I'm not participating in this ridiculousness.

SOPHIE

Fine. Here is your orange blanket.

JACOB

Was that so hard?

SOPHIE

Now we have to venture through the mystical Montañas de Carne.

JACOB

What?

SOPHIE

The mystical Meat Mountains.

JACOB

That's not a real thing.

SOPHIE

To get your turkey sandwich.

JACOB

Why can't I just order it from the menu?

SOPHIE

What's the fun in that?

JACOB

What fun are MEAT MOUNTAINS? Don't they like . . . smell? Or feel weird? Where did they find that much meat?

SOPHIE

Fine, fine. Ok, the last thing we need to find on the magic map is the TV remote.

JACOB

I think you hid it, EXPLORA, so we could play this wacked out game and you could distract me while you put the IV in.

SOPHIE

[*In a normal voice; Explora is gone.*] Did it work?

JACOB

No, STABBER NO STABBING.

SOPHIE

Jacob, I have to put the needle in.

JACOB

No. STABBER NO STABBING. STABBER NO STABBING. Say it with me pretend TV audience my crazy nurse is talking to. STABBER NO STABBING.

SOPHIE

I'll be very careful.

JACOB

Nope.

SOPHIE

You aren't going to make this into a battle are you?

JACOB

Yes. Yes, if I have to, I am going to battle you.

SOPHIE

Really.

JACOB

Every year I'm in the *Nutcracker*, well ALMOST every year, COVID ruined it for a while, and the last time I was a mouse in the Mouse King number and I know how this goes.

SOPHIE

Really?

JACOB

Yes.

[*He pulls out a kazoo. He starts humming the* Nutcracker *music into it.*]

SOPHIE

Where did you get that kazoo?

[*She pulls one out too.*]

JACOB

Where did *you* get that kazoo?

SOPHIE

Oh so you'll imagine now?

JACOB

I don't know what you're talking about.

SOPHIE

Ok fine. So you're the Mouse King?

JACOB

No! I'm the Nutcracker and YOU'RE the Mouse King.

SOPHIE

Really?

JACOB

Yes. Cause you're evil and shouldn't be here and have a sword!

SOPHIE

I have a sword?

JACOB

No. Not a sword. I have the sword. You have . . . a giant needle!

SOPHIE

Oh really?

JACOB

Yes! And you're trying to stab me with it.

SOPHIE

Like this?

> [*Suddenly she does have a giant syringe. She advances on him with the needle. A ballet dance battle ensues, it goes on for several minutes. There are pirouettes and jetés and grand battements. Which is pronounced just NOTHING like it is spelled.* JACOB /

THE NUTCRACKER *gets a sword. He dance fights with* SOPHIE / THE MOUSE KING *in a massive battle. For a moment it seems like he might defeat* THE MOUSE KING, *he's very strong and very determined. But he's got a kazoo, and a sword, AND he's doing ballet and it's too much.* JACOB / THE NUTCRACKER *falters. He collapses to the ground, kazoo and sword abandoned, breathing hard.* THE MOUSE KING *is stronger.* THE MOUSE KING *wins!* THE MOUSE KING *stands over* JACOB *with her giant needle.*]

SOPHIE

I win!

JACOB

The Mouse King NEVER wins.

SOPHIE

Well, I did this time.

JACOB

I have been in this ballet three years, every year but the last one, since I was eight. The Nutcracker always wins!

SOPHIE

This time it's the Mouse King! Now you have to let me put the IV in.

JACOB

No! No, no, no! It's NOT FAIR. The only reason you won is because I'm so weak because I'm sick.

SOPHIE

I know.

JACOB

None of this is fair.

SOPHIE

I know.

JACOB

I hurt all the time. I lost so much weight. I was so tired. I couldn't even play soccer anymore. I had to change schools because my teachers didn't understand why I had to spend so much time in the bathroom. They thought I was trying to skip class. I used to LOVE going to school. I wasn't skipping class on purpose! I'm scared to go places in public. What if I need the bathroom? It doesn't feel safe.

SOPHIE

I know. And if you let me put the medicine in, it should help you get back to ballet and maybe spend less time in the bathroom and feel not so tired.

JACOB

I still don't trust you.

SOPHIE

I promise I'm on your side, Jacob.

JACOB

People who are on your side don't hurt you.

SOPHIE

I'm a nurse because I want to help kids. I know that sometimes nurses don't get it right the first time and that isn't fair.

JACOB

My mom told them last time after the third time they poked me that if they didn't get it right the fourth time we were leaving. Let me show you how it went. Sitcom flashback time!!

SOPHIE

Sitcom flashback time?

JACOB

I've been streaming these super old sitcoms. Like *Math Nerds and the Blonde Lady* or *Pals.*

SOPHIE

Those are super old? Just hand me a cane and bifocals and stick me in the old folks home now I guess.

JACOB

I mean they're from like the 1900s right? And they have these over-the-top laugh tracks? Like no matter what the characters say the audience DIES laughing. Wait. Let me show you. Say what you just said and our LIVE STUDIO AUDIENCE will crack up. Ready everyone? Ok, say it.

SOPHIE

Just hand me a cane and bifocals and stick me in the old folks' home now I guess?

JACOB

EVERYBODY LAUGH AS LOUD AS YOU CAN! That was great. Ok, so here is how it went. In this flashback, you will be my bumbling nurse and I will still be me. Do the flashback hands with me please.

SOPHIE

The flashback hands?

JACOB

Like this.

> [*You can invent these or use the ones like those from* Wayne's World. *Everybody does the flashback hands.*]

SOPHIE

Hi, I'm . . . Nurse Scratchandsniff Clutterbunk . . . [JACOB *has sourced a "Laugh" sign and holds it up.*] and I'm here to put your IV needle in.

JACOB

What an unusual name, Nurse . . .

SOPHIE

Clutterbunk. [JACOB *holds up Laugh sign.*] It's Hungarian. Which is perfect because I am always HUNGARY! [*Laugh sign.*] Ok, that was really not that funny.

JACOB

Doesn't matter, you hold the sign, the laughter flows. Like magnificent vocal lava.

[*The sign.*]

SOPHIE

Ok, so I'm going to stick the needle in your arm. This will only hurt a WHOLE GOSH DARN LOT.

[*Do it.*]

JACOB

Wait wait wait . . . no thank you. That doesn't sound fun at all.

SOPHIE

Well, how do we do the medicine if we don't stick it in your arm? Ok, so just give me the arm you want me to use.

JACOB

How about no arm if it's going to hurt a lot?

SOPHIE

Ok, I'll just use a leg!

[SOPHIE *grabs* JACOB*'s leg and he's hopping around on stage. He turns an awkward pirouette.*]

JACOB

I might be a dancer but I don't like this tango!

[*Sign time.*]

SOPHIE

Could I BE ANY MORE bad at this?

JACOB

Well you could be, if you were wearing a blindfold and I spun YOU around four times!

SOPHIE

Come on Jacob it's NEEDLE TIME.

JACOB

Are you really a nurse? Because at this point I think YOU'RE THREE ANGRY CATS IN SCRUBS.

[*Laugh sign.*]

SOPHIE

[*Breaking character.*] Ok, ok, I get it. It did not go well.

JACOB

You can say that again.

SOPHIE

Ok, ok, I get it. It did not go well. [*Sign time.*] I just wanted one more go with that. But seriously . . . the flashback has gone on long enough. I get the point.

JACOB

Well so did I, like four times because of that nurse. [*Sign time.*] Did they pay those audiences or something? Because it's only been like three minutes and I am completely tired of laughing.

SOPHIE

Flashback hands please everyone. [*Everyone does flashback hands so we are in the present.*] I promise, I promise I am way better at needles than Nurse Scratchandsniff Clutterbunk. Which is a ridiculous name. Did you just make that up?

JACOB

Totally.

SOPHIE

You're pretty funny, Jacob, even without a laugh track. And I told you imagination would help. But I really need to go get your medicine, I promise it will be ok.

JACOB

Well we just locked eyes so you can't leave.

SOPHIE

What are you talking about?

JACOB

I am using my imagination. Just like you TOLD me to. And I am imagining we are Pokedude trainers and if two Pokedude trainers lock eyes, they have to battle!

SOPHIE

Oh really.

JACOB

And if you don't do this, I will know everything you said about imagination was a lie.

SOPHIE

I am going to get in a lot of trouble for how slow I am today. I don't think they deduct flashbacks from my time per patient.

JACOB

Oh well.

SOPHIE

Ok, explain to me, how you get to be a Pokedude trainer.

[JACOB *gets out of his bed. He slings the orange blanket around his back like a cape.*]

JACOB

Ok, so the goal is to battle your Pokedudes, and defeat the other trainer's. If I were a Pokedude trainer, like Pine, he's the main character, I wouldn't always have the same weak Pokedudes. As soon as he gets a strong one, he lets it go the very same episode. It's a terrible strategy. I would catch a . . . Curtle.

SOPHIE

A Curtle?

JACOB

It's half cat, half turtle. All stealth.

SOPHIE

This isn't fair . . . I don't know this show. Audience, do you know the show Jacob is pretending? [*She waits for the audience.*] You do? What Pokedude should I use? [*Listens to answers.*]

JACOB

Who are you talking to? This isn't *Explora*! There's nobody to talk to!

SOPHIE

Ok fine, I think I get this anyway. I shall use the power of my new Llamahog to capture your Curtle and it shall be mine.

JACOB

It's evil team Spaceship! You'll never get my Curtle! Wait. What's a Llamahog.

SOPHIE

Half Llama. Half Hedgehog. It's spiky and it spits acid. And it's definitely stronger than yours.

JACOB

No it isn't.

SOPHIE

How is a half cat, half turtle dangerous? Like, at ALL? Doesn't it just nap all day?

JACOB

Just because something needs to sleep a lot, doesn't make it weak or defenseless. My Curtle has a tough shell that can repel spikes and it can do a shell spin and take out all FOUR of your Llamahog's feet.

SOPHIE

[*Mocking Jacob.*] And after it does a spin, does it have to rest for a year?

JACOB

It used to, but then I gave it a special infusion that made it evolve to be really strong again. There's no way you can beat us.

SOPHIE

In your dreams! Let's battle! Llamahog shoot spikes!

JACOB

Curtle! Use defensive shell!

SOPHIE

Ha ha! Defensive shell? That will never stop my acid spit! And the acid spit will make you sicker and sicker and then you won't be able to do anything.

JACOB

I TOLD you, we evolved so the spit doesn't hurt as much. Curtle use shell spin! Go for its legs!

SOPHIE

Get back up Llamahog! Ha ha! My Llamahog has defeated you! Your Pokedude has fainted.

JACOB

That's what you think. It's half cat. So it has 4.5 lives! Curtle DEFEATS Llamahog.

SOPHIE

Oh dear.

JACOB

And we LAUNCH YOU INTO SPACE. Like the ALIEN I always knew you were.

SOPHIE

[*Trying to leave the room.*] I'm blasting off again!

JACOB

Sophie! Sophie! Wait, please don't leave. Please.

SOPHIE

Jacob, you can't stall forever. I do have other patients. I need to get you going with your drip so I can help other kids.

JACOB

You told me I have a big imagination. But it's not big enough. I can use my imagination to pretend I'm in TV shows or that I'm from space but you know what I really want to pretend and can't?

SOPHIE

What?

JACOB

That I'm me but not sick. Ever.

SOPHIE

Yeah.

JACOB

It feels normal to be sick now. My normal.

SOPHIE

That must be hard.

JACOB

It's hard because there aren't enough bathrooms. Or enough time. I spend so much time being sick, so much time with my stomach hurting, I miss out on things I love. And I can't imagine being a kid who never worries about being sick and missing things. And I can try to explain, but I can't find the words.

SOPHIE

Is that why you love ballet, because you don't need words to show how you feel?

JACOB

When I can be in ballet with my friends I have a really good time.

SOPHIE

What is that like?

JACOB

Here.

[*He hands her a kazoo.*]

SOPHIE

Where do you keep getting those?

JACOB

Play something sad. I'll show you.

[SOPHIE *plays the kazoo.* JACOB *dances a solo. It is not technically complicated or perfect. He might mess up sometimes. But it's a dance of hurting. Of being sad. Of feeling alone. Of worry. But while he dances it, he smiles.*]

SOPHIE

That was beautiful Jacob.

JACOB

Thank you. But I hope really soon I get to dance it for other people, instead of just you.

SOPHIE

I hope you get to dance it really soon too. I hope you get to do all kinds of things. Like go to camp, and play soccer, and make friends with other people like you so you can complain about your stabby nurses. Hey, can I show you a magic trick?

JACOB

Sure.

SOPHIE

Hold up your orange blanket so you can't see me.

JACOB

Ok. [*He does.*] I try not to cry or to complain but I complain inside. A lot.

SOPHIE

Yeah.

JACOB

And my mom can always tell. I'm sad I make my parents worry.

SOPHIE

It's normal that they worry. I'm glad you have parents who really care about you. We all need someone who pays attention to us. So guess what?

JACOB

What?

SOPHIE

While we were talking, I already put the needle in.

JACOB

No way.

SOPHIE

Yep. I figured if you weren't looking it wouldn't be so bad.

JACOB

I knew what you were doing.

SOPHIE

I know you did. You're a brave kid. Here's the remote. I'll be back in a bit to check on you.

JACOB

Is this going to take as long as last time? Last time we got here in the morning and it was NIGHT when we left.

SOPHIE

I'm afraid so. Maybe a little bit longer this time because you are such a fierce warrior in battle.

JACOB

You are good at putting in needles.

SOPHIE

I told you.

JACOB

Why aren't all the nurses as good at it?

SOPHIE

They didn't train on Mars like I did.

JACOB

Hah hah.

SOPHIE

I'll be back in a little bit to check on you.

JACOB

Ok. I wish I brought a DVD to pass the time.

SOPHIE

You should do that next time, so you're not stuck with shows like *Explora.*

JACOB

Honestly, that was kind of fun. This time was way better than last time Sophie.

SOPHIE

Well, you knew what to expect this time. Things always seem a lot scarier if you've never done them before. And you distracted yourself. By imagining.

JACOB

And that's what grown-ups do?

SOPHIE

How would I know what grown-up earth humans do? [*Back to her alien voice.*] I told you, I am Xenu 16 from the planet Mars.